BLESSED
ARE THE
BANK
ROBBERS

Also by the Author:

Welcome to Paradise, Now Go to Hell

Cocaine + Surfing

Reports from Hell

BLESSED ARE THE BANK ROBBERS

THE <u>TRUE</u> ADVENTURES
OF AN EVANGELICAL OUTLAW

CHAS SMITH

ABRAMS PRESS, NEW YORK

Library of Congress Control Number: 2021946851

ISBN: 978-1-4197-5473-9
eISBN: 978-1-64700-546-7

Printed and bound in the Unites States
10 9 8 7 6 5 4 3 2 1

ABRAMS The Art of Books
195 Broadway, New York, NY 10007
abramsbooks.com

CONTENTS

"What the world requires of the Christians
is that they continue to be Christians."
—Albert Camus

"Love God and sin boldly."
—Martin Luther

CHAPTER 1

WELCOME TO PARADISE

So there I was in the front yard, one sun-dappled spring morning, scolding my daughter's Chihuahua, Thunderstruck, for getting into my wife's gluten-free crackers again, when the mail jalopy came rumbling to a stop in front of the driveway. The postman, a bro, seemed happy to chat while handing me an assortment of mail.

"You surf today?"

"No, but heard it was blown out. Probably get on it later, though, if it glasses."

"Cool."

He drove off with a shaka, leaving a puff of diesel smoke in his wake, Thunder seizing on the moment to scamper back inside, dang dog. If she's gonna get naughty, she should do better than gluten-free.

I flipped through the small stack. A DMV renewal, an overdue physical therapy bill, a letter from the Federal Detention Center/Federal Correctional Institution Englewood—and paused, electric rush flooding from head to toe, ending in my tingling fingertips.

This was what I'd been waiting for, semipatiently, like I used to wait for the Sears Christmas catalog. Letting the unnecessary mail drop, I wandered over to the patio, pulled out a black chair, and sat down, wondering what Littleton, Colorado, feels like in late March while studying the envelope.

Daniel Courson 19560023

Federal Detention Center/Federal Correctional

Institution Englewood

9595 West Quincy Ave.

Littleton, CO 80123

The blue ink hovered above and to the left of my own Cardiff-by-the-Sea address. Daniel Courson 19560023. My Cousin Danny.

I had asked him to write every bit of his experience, seeing that he had nothing but time stretching out over that Rocky Mountain horizon, seeing that he had taken the adventurous life to a critical new level. I told him I'd critique because, selfishly, I needed every last detail. I'd waited patiently, and now here it was.

The envelope's flap peeled open easily enough, a byproduct of prison censors or maybe just lower-quality prison commissary stationary, and I skimmed the introduction. "Hey Charlie, greetings from Colorado, my final destination after a tour of the western US courtesy of your US tax dollars, so thanks for that. Rod Blagojevich, the Illinois senator who sold his senate seat, is here as well as Jared, the old pitchman for Subway who was involved in child porn, I believe."

Rod Blagojevich had actually been Illinois's governor and had tried to sell Barack Obama's vacated senate seat. He has Subway's Jared Fogle correctly pegged though, or mostly: fifteen years plus eight months for possessing child pornography and traveling across state lines to pay for sex with minors.

I knew that on his stop through Nevada, Cousin Danny had shared a cell with Cliven Bundy, the lightning rod Oregon rancher who led an armed standoff with the Bureau of Land Management, reaching hero status among radicalized libertarians, the two trading stories while whittling away the hours. He had also spent time in the depressing cement box once occupied by Oklahoma City bomber Timothy McVeigh in Denver, the prison guard informing him of its famous ex-tenant while locking the door for the night in an offhanded but proud way.

After a few more general pleasantries, elucidations of prison politics, and a request to "read and give feedback," I remember that this is serious and run upstairs, fish my fancy, serious-editing Montblanc from a desk drawer packed with LOL OMG doll clothes, run back downstairs, and tuck in properly.

CHAPTER 1

Bank robbery was starting to get boring. After forty-some jobs, I was beginning to think I'd seen it all. But I'd read enough online news stories of the jobs gone wrong, failed by an X factor: off-duty cop in line, hero armed customer, goddam GPS trackers . . . it was easy to be unlucky. Still, that didn't stop me from getting back to work. I decided the next bank needed some extra attention. Instead of the usual casing from within a Starbucks or McDonald's across the street, this time I'd gear up like a construction worker . . . a large work site encircled this bank—some kind of revamped parking lot was being installed and workers buzzed around everywhere. Perfect cover.

So, with my hard hat, orange safety vest, work boots, and gloves, I sidled up the sidewalk and edged into the churned-up earth just outside the bank, bending over some imaginary task. My dark safety glasses hid my sideways glances at the arriving bank staff: one, two, three, four office and teller workers, no hero ex-military bearings to be found.

Bingo.

I made a couple more trips in my disguise to the work site during the week, checking the flow of customers, timing my escape route, spacing cop patrols.

Friday is the optimal day to rob a bank. It's the day people with actual jobs come to cash paychecks, so banks need the maximum amount of cash on hand.

The morning of the robbery was crisp and clear, and after plenty of strong coffee in my cup I again donned my Village People getup with one important addition—that old standby in bank robber couture, the black mask pulled down around my neck ready for use.

I parked my pickup a few blocks away and quickly hoisted my full-suspension Trek mountain bike from the truck bed to under my feet. My backpack hugged my body, only two items inside: a realistic-looking Glock pellet gun and a hammer, both tools of last resort. The gun's presence to frighten, the hammer's purpose being to smash glass doors locking me in.

The excuses flooded my brain as I pedaled between buildings, along paths, toward the target.

"Too much traffic."

"Not enough traffic."

"Cops could be close."

"Something doesn't feel right."

Still I pedaled, fighting fear, fighting anxiety. "Do this. Make it happen. Just get it over with."

I rode right up to the bank entrance, past the morning swarm of similarly dressed workers. Not a second glance my way. I leaned my bike against a bank wall.

Now, the moment, the border between nothing and everything, my throat tight with invisible hands squeezing, sweat trickling down my back. Same drenching of forced anticipation every time.

"Fuck it."

Oh, man.

I scribbled my first note in the prison paper margins. "Lose 'goddam.'" Even poorly spelled it clangs off my soul, and it must have clanged off Cousin Danny's soul too.

My second note, more a curiosity, is why he is writing as a hard-bitten East Coast Italian-American mafioso bank robber starting to get bored, looking out for hero and/or military armed customers, goddamn GPS trackers, construction worker getups, casing, bingo, Village People, fuck it?

Cousin Danny, like me, is not an East Coast Italian-American or even an East Coast Irish-American but rather the dictionary definition of West Coast WASP. Tall, thin, blue-eyed, almost brown hair that turns blond with enough surfing, an Anglo-Saxon genetic mixture that is neither fancy nor interesting. Just white. He grew up in Carlsbad, named after a mineral spa town in the Czech Republic, a stone's throw from my now Cardiff-by-the-Sea address, named after the Welsh capital, a short hop north from San Diego. "America's Finest City."

We used to boogie board Warm Water Jetty, a beach that had a power plant spewing warmer water back into the ocean, after it had been sucked into cool turbines or whatnot, then made drip sandcastles with warm sand when my family drove down for summer vacations from perpetually gray, cold, windy, depressed Coos Bay, Oregon. Or go to the local surf shop, Carlsbad Pipelines, where I would press my nose against the glass counter, carefully selecting the two stickers I was allowed, inhaling the coconut scent of Sex Wax while trying to not get caught looking at the word "sex."

I hated my hometown.

Oh, my parents were wonderful, generous, kind. They both worked extremely hard to give us—my older sister and younger brother, great siblings—everything they could. Looking back, it was a storybook existence. Our house, perched on a high hill, overlooked Coos Bay's port, and I would sit in big bay windows and watch tugboats putter around, pedal my bike down rain-slicked streets to Mingus Park, where our half–German shepherd half-collie would get in big trouble for killing ducks underneath towering Douglas fir trees. But it was not California, and I was convinced that I was a Californian, a *Southern* Californian, so I hated the gray, the rain, the freezing ocean water, the green.

Hated it enough to fantasize about someday buying a B-1 bomber, stacking it with World War II surplus bombs, flying into

Coos Bay's airspace, and laying waste to the coast from Bandon to Florence.

Unlike me, Cousin Danny didn't just romanticize criminal binges but actually carried one out, and on a legendary scale. *Is* carrying one out on a legendry scale, even though momentarily stalled behind bars. He has to be within spitting distance of the US record for bank robberies and probably the world record too: forty-some and counting, I don't know exactly, nobody does, because bank robbery is a proper dark art. Some bandits take credit for banks they didn't rob. Others don't cop to a full total. There's no real cross-checking over state lines, and many unsolved cases get left off the books due to lack of evidence.

Forty-some and counting, though, is near the top, and Cousin Danny sorted out how to rob banks at a record-setting pace, all while having to learn how to be a criminal on the fly, all on his own, seeing that underworld behavior was not part of our upbringing.

We were the dictionary definition of West Coast WASP, yes, but imbued with a spiritual heritage second to none. The Coursons, you see, are one of the legendary families in modern evangelical Christianity. Megachurch pastors and renowned missionaries appearing regularly on the Trinity Broadcasting Network. Radio stations around the world broadcasting Courson sermons. Books written by them, books written about them. Courson Bible commentaries flying off the shelves of Christian bookstores. Tens of thousands of weekly worshipers coming to hear Coursons preach live, hundreds of thousands more following virtually. A gilded evangelical Christian Camelot—and learning how to launder money, much less curse, was not part of the upbringing.

Most recently, Cousin Danny was grabbed after taking a Tinder date named Lynette—decidedly not evangelical Christian behavior—to a night of local author readings at a trendy indoor-outdoor bar. Drinking bespoke whiskey cocktails around firepits on a warm spring night, chatting with Tinder-adjacent friends, wearing shorts, with many in the crowd wearing sport sandals.

The arresting SWAT team shot a flash-bang grenade at him on his way out with Lynette, a personal trainer, then stood around high-fiving each other once he was bloodied and secured in the back of a cop SUV. One showed him a picture pulled from the internet, demanding to know, "Is this you?" before taking in his tall, thin, blue-eyed, almost-brown hair that would have turned blond if he had chosen to hide on the coast and saying, "Yeah. It's you."

Danny had been a fugitive on the run from the FBI for three years prior, robbing banks throughout the western United States. Staying a few steps ahead by scouring the darknet for tips, purchasing fake IDs, attaching pirated credit cards to those fake IDs, using cryptocurrency to buy fake license plates for his Toyota Tacoma (that was marked as stolen in law enforcement databases), driving it to Kansas for a shopping spree on pirated credit cards to throw the FBI off the scent as per industry standard, etc.

They almost got him a few times, of course, before they actually got him again. Most recently after a bank job in Boulder, Colorado, where he ordered the tellers, "No dye packs, no GPS, top two drawers, fast!" like some hard-bitten gangster.

Apparently, the last teller didn't obey, and Cousin Danny had cop cars on his Tacoma well before they should have been. Or maybe those cop cars were there because Danny had hit the same bank a few weeks earlier, netting more than $50,000 by having those same tellers open the day vault. His largest single-day haul. In any case, a phalanx of cop cars, sirens blaring, close enough where he could make out their white knuckles gripping steering wheels. Furrowed brows and wraparound black sunglasses.

Drenched in panic sweat, Danny threw his duffel bag stuffed with ill-gotten cash out the window, watched the bills make a mushroom cloud behind him, fluttering into the air, then punched it through a red-light intersection into a suburban neighborhood, knowing that the cops wouldn't endanger the lives of young Colorado boys playing catch with their fathers the way he would.

It worked.

The cops backed off, and he made it to his cash-upfront rental room with minutes to clean up and get all the way out. Johnny Law had too much information now. A description of his vehicle, DNA from the duffel bag, the bicycle he used for his initial getaways (covered in more DNA), and smiling shirtless cell phone snaps thanks to his Denver Tinder girlfriend, to whom he had confessed that he was not, in fact, Scott Hopkins but rather Daniel David Courson, a bank-robbing fugitive on the run.

He did not want to go back to prison, that much he knew. Did not want those "vacuous eyes of lifers" he had witnessed during his first eight-year stretch for bank robbery in California. Didn't want to brawl for his life, again, in a concrete box, blood splattered everywhere, or deal with the un-woke strictures of race relations behind bars.

They'd throw the book at him, for sure, and he would spend the rest of his days behind bars, navigating a world of rage and hate that people with Cousin Danny's pedigree only experience via the "saved" ex-convict who comes to warn kids off crime and chasing the "lusts of the flesh" in evangelical youth group.

He hated prison. Hated the food, the air, the guards, the daily humiliation—though he occasionally enjoyed the company of his fellow outlaws. When being moved to a new prison, or left in a holding cell before heading to court, he'd have to cough up that he was in for bank robbery lest a tattoo-free, clean-cut, well-educated mid-forties white man like him get fingered as a chomo. Like Jared Fogle. On those occasions, he would also have to cough up tricks of his trade—getaway secrets, money-laundering details—while other inmates took careful mental notes.

Word of Cousin Danny's almost-successful escape usually preceded him as well, further smoothing the way. He had used his medical knowledge to fake appendicitis, get taken to a local hospital and prepped for surgery. While one of his guards was getting coffee, he pretended that he was soiling himself, got his other guard to unshackle him and take him to the bathroom, where he spun and sprinted down the emergency room hallway, prison-issue sandals slapping the cold tile, shocked gasps and screams all around. He made it out into the parking lot, down the street, and into an alley before getting jumped from behind by two San Diego State University track stars who happened to be working the night shift as hospital orderlies.

The luck.

He had been awaiting trial after hitting nineteen banks during a torrid six-week summer stretch—sometimes two banks in one day, a bank after he picked up dinner groceries or a bank during his lunch break. He was a physician's assistant, mostly helping replace knees at Scripps hospital, with an estranged, soon-to-officially-be-ex wife and their seven-year-old son waiting intermittently for "visiting days with Daddy." Nineteen banks, a full-time high-stress job, broken marriage, freshly discovered blackjack hobby, and a T-ball coaching gig to boot.

The police caught him that first time on the way to work one hot morning, grinding him into the cement, tearing and bloodying his scrubs, sending practice baseballs bouncing into a suburban north county San Diego neighborhood, shouting directly into his skull, "We've got you, motherfucker!" And "Why do you have so many baseballs, motherfucker?"

Danny's first lawyer told him he was looking at twenty-years-plus. He couldn't imagine getting out when his son was in his late twenties, so he tried to escape. Would have escaped if it wasn't for those meddling collegiate track stars.

In the end, though, he was only given eight years, seeing that he had not used a gun and had no record, also being the dictionary definition of West Coast WASP, serving just under, and would have been around for his son's entire high school experience, maybe even the last months of junior high, if he hadn't decided to pull an art-and-jewel heist while still on probation, only three months a free man. He was caught mid-job, but made it away, driving east into the night, the life of a fugitive stretching over his stolen Toyota Tacoma's dashboard, defining his near future.

"How in the world did you start robbing banks?" I had asked him during that first lockup in a dusty yet somehow shiny cement prison overlooking the US-Mexico border.

He didn't answer me then, as we were both distracted by Sirhan Sirhan, Robert F. Kennedy's convicted murderer, coming into the spartan visiting room, but he wrote a few weeks later.

> How does someone get to the point of standing over a
> teller, waiting for her shaking hands to pile the money
> on the marble counter? In my case, it began with a white
> picket fence. Or, more specifically, hammering the last
> white post into the ground, looking around the tract
> cul-de-sac, and realizing that the wide-eyed dreams of
> suburban middle-class bliss were bullshit.

Oh, man.

Bullshit is right.

The "realization that generic suburban bliss ain't all that it's cracked up to be" is a trope so tired, so lazy, as to demand dismissal from anyone even half literate, but mostly, it's absolutely not true. The seed of Cousin Danny's bank robbing, I'm convinced, was planted while sitting cross-legged on the carpeted floor of the tiny loft in his parents' faux-Tudor Carlsbad home, his brother Mikey; my sister Emily and brother Andy there too; his mom, my Aunt Kris, downstairs making Jiffy Pop; his dad, my Uncle Dave, readying the night's entertainment. An edifying, uplifting, inspiring, and thoroughly engrossing evangelical missionary slideshow. A visual representation of the bigger-than-life Courson adventure we were all living. The same bigger-than-life Courson adventure, slightly twisted, with a dash here and a sprinkle there, that creates a bank robber.

CHAPTER 2

UNCLE DAVE

When I was born, we lived in San Jose—in my childhood imagination an earthly paradise of sun and culture—but then my mom's dad, Grampy, got a bank president job in Coos Bay, moved, and lured my parents with the region's distinctive rot. Having just turned three, I was too young to protest. My father got a job teaching English at Marshfield High School, they bought that house perched high on a hill in town, and my rotten attitude began to percolate, completely unnecessarily, in my dreamed-up Southern Californian heart.

My grandparents' moss-covered, shake-roofed home was a fantastic respite, though, from the never-ending gray. It smelled of potpourri and fresh batches of Chex mix, had a hot tub I wasn't allowed to use, bay windows where I watched ships laden with woodchips ferrying out to the open Pacific, and a bumper pool table I only realized was not "real" pool until very much later in life.

They had a backyard garden ringed with rhododendron, a greenhouse, and a private trail down to a small beach littered with driftwood and the occasional glass ball float. We'd spend many gray days on their beach, sometimes with Cousin Danny and Cousin Mikey when they were up, poking sea anemones in the tide pools, getting pinched by crabs, spearing them in the back with driftwood.

When it began raining too hard, we'd move inside, but Nana had strict rules, like no using the hot tub, no goofing around with the Madame Alexander dolls, and no messing up the felt on the bumper pool table, so I'd often find myself staring at her pictures tacked onto the wall. My young mother getting dropped off at Bible college, fiery red hair cut into a chic flip, the very image of mid-1960s Kingston Trio cleanliness with a touch of Peter, Paul and Mary thrown in for flare. Uncle Jonny, brown leather Bible in hand, fiery red beard covering his face, fiery red hair capping it off, preaching to a small gathering under a tree. Uncle Jim, already bald at twenty, standing next to a fiery red convertible MG. Uncle Dave, the firstborn, standing in some Vietnam jungle clearing with fellow marines, draped in camouflage, camouflaged bucket hat over heavy Marine-issue black-rimmed glasses, M16 slung over a shoulder, smiling his broad crooked smile that mirrored my own.

I first became aware of Uncle Dave from staring at those pictures. Those were my favorite, and I studied them for hours, wondering what Uncle Dave had seen, what he'd done, how it smelled, tasted, felt to be part of a war. A war in a faraway, exotic land. A war against fiery red Communism, that godless ideology dead set on destroying religion around the world, and especially evangelical Christianity.

Uncle Dave had dropped out of Bible college to enlist in the Marine Corps during the bloodiest years of the Vietnam War, and served as a gunnery sergeant in the demilitarized zone. I'd naively ask Nana if he ever killed anyone. She'd answer tersely that we don't ask those sorts of questions. I'd ask Uncle Dave when we visited. He'd laugh while pivoting. I'd ask my mom, and she would say she didn't know because she either really didn't or had a solid poker face. Not that killing people was valuable, important, or good, but it fascinated me, and the fact that it was never talked about made it all the more fascinating. Uncle Dave didn't seem like the sort who would kill people.

After coming home, he planted a church with his brother, Uncle Jonny, in San Jose. Their partnership did not last long, though that wasn't talked about either, and then he founded Christian Emergency Relief Team, or CERT, in Carlsbad.

The organization's mission was to run much-needed medical supplies and doctors into crisis situations before *Médecins Sans Frontières* or the United Nations arrived. I devoured each and every one of his stories, leading his elite physician unit through conflict-ravaged Honduras, civil-war-thrashed Beirut, and the lightly battered Falklands, stitching wounds, pulling rotten teeth, building churches, handing out Bibles. Or, when not overseas, leading inspiring prayer breakfasts in Washington, DC, in order to raise support for vulnerable communities around the world where the soil was right to receive the gospel.

In my mind, Uncle Dave was a cross between Indiana Jones and Paul the Apostle. A swashbuckling tall, thin, blue-eyed hero with a crooked smile and almost-brown hair that turns blond with enough sun cutting through exotic jungles, sidestepping deadly land mines, shaking hands with brave Republicans.

I would wear my red CERT T-shirt around Coos Bay with such pride and look forward to when we visited him and his boys, my Cousins Danny and Mikey, or when he visited us, usually on a church tour, sharing stories from the field. "You know, Charlie . . ." he would say in his distinctive, slow, hyper-enunciated way, ". . . we were there in the jungles of Honduras with the *Mis-ki-to* peoples, bringing them malaria medicine and the gospel." Or "You know, Charlie . . . we were there in the jungles of Nicaragua with the *May-ang-na* peoples, bringing them important dental care and the gospel."

When I was six years old, my father decided to teach in a missionary school in the small town of Ukarumpa up in the highlands of Papua New Guinea. I spent two merciful years outside of Coos Bay's gray, pedaling my bike around the red-dirt roads with my best friend, whose father was a missionary helicopter pilot.

Uncle Dave came to visit and led a group, including my father, deep into the surrounding jungle, where the cannibals lived, bringing important dental care and the gospel. When they came home, over a week later, his eyes were on fire with stories of impossible danger, and also malaria. Swinging over rivers swollen with man-eating saltwater crocodiles. Dinners with cannibals who had actually tasted other men.

I hung on every word.

And there, sitting cross-legged on the carpeted floor of the tiny loft in his faux-Tudor Carlsbad home, sandwiched between Cousins Danny and Mikey, digging into the just-burst Jiffy Pop foil, Uncle Dave dropping the final slides into the carousel, I was beyond excited. This was entertainment. Edifying, inspiring, real entertainment only beaten, maybe, by movies about Christians escaping communist East Germany by hot-air balloon.

The lights were dimmed, the machine whirred to life spitting its hot air into the already hot room, and the first image flashed on the white wall. There was Uncle Dave, except he wasn't wearing his typical missionary costume—shorts, hiking boots, CERT T-shirt—but rather a full beard, funny hat, and long dress-like shirt standing next to a laden donkey and two men who were dressed the same as him holding impressive rifles in some snowy moonscape.

"Those are *muj-a-hi-deen*," Uncle Dave hyper-enunciated. "Freedom Fighters. And the donkey is carrying Stinger missiles that we are taking over the *Khy-ber* Pass into Afghanistan so these men and their families can fall in love with Jesus."

The slideshow continued, and I was intoxicated, learning how the mujahideen were fighting the godless Communists, and their technological superiority, with turn-of-the-century muskets.

"The Soviet armed forces, a powerful military, will fly helicopters into the steep valleys that cut through the Hindu Kush mountains, lured by small bands of mujahideen. Their brothers hide high in the cliffs above, and when the helicopters begin their descent to hunt those below, they shoot lead balls from their muskets that stick to the helicopters' blades, throw off the balance, and bring them down."

It sounded like a miracle straight out of the Old Testament. Like the vastly outnumbered Israelites defeating the Philistines. Like David, wearing his simple shepherd's clothes, slinging a stone at a well-armored giant, killing him and destroying the stronger enemy's will.

Mujahideen! Freedom Fighters! Smashing the Evil Empire with sheer moxie! With muskets and now American-made Stinger missiles! Slide after slide depicting striking, bearded men with fierce eyes, Uncle Dave in their midst, charred helicopter skeletons, whole trains of donkeys, snow, mountains, Uncle Dave not smiling.

My jaw was on the floor when the lights came back on. Uncle Dave had already completely captured my imagination, with Vietnam and the jungles of Central America, but now he was my hero, he was what I wanted to grow up and be. I looked at Cousins Danny and Mikey, who both appeared slightly bored by their father's stories, especially Cousin Mikey. I looked at my sister, Emily, who had plastered her "family polite" look on before the slideshow and was having trouble shaking it now. I looked at my brother, Andy, who was banging a drum riff from Christian rock band Petra on his knees. How could they not all be as visibly thrilled as me? Adventure, wild adventure, in the most excitingly unhinged package ever. They had no imaginations, no literary sense—in retrospect, though, I was misreading Cousin Danny's bored look and misreading it badly. The seed was there, planted and growing.

I stuttered a few questions to Uncle Dave, mind still ablaze, then was shuttled back downstairs to look at boogie board magazines with Cousin Mikey so the adults could talk. Cousin Danny had some studying to do, or reading, or something nerdy by himself in his room. He, the firstborn of all the cousins, was also considered the smartest. My sister, the second-born, ran a close second in terms of brains, having had read the entire Little Women series before fourth grade, but Cousin Danny was in a whole other class, being good at math, and was certainly in line to become an astronaut, according to Nana, or at least one of the Navy's Top Guns if his desirable tallness got in the way of space travel. Cousin Mikey, the third-born, was very good at boogie boarding, had trained his parrot to speak, and had a rabbit, so was certainly going to be a renowned zoologist or famous professional boogie boarder. My brother Andy, down at seventh-born, could keep rhythm along with every Christian rock band, from Adam Again to Zion, so was clearly on his way to fortune and renown in Christian rock circles. I, born a nondescript fifth, not apparently smart, certainly not good at math, was going to be Uncle Dave. A marine then a missionary who would adventurously save the very world.

On the way down to Cousin Mikey's room, I passed framed pictures that I had passed many times before, hanging on the stairway wall. Uncle Dave and Aunt Kris, young, with longer hair, having just gotten married. Baby pictures of Cousin Danny and Cousin Mikey, standard issue, diapered, laying on a green lawn. Uncle Dave, in a fine blue suit, smiling his crooked smile standing next to an important official dressed in fancy military greens.

I stopped, mind still blazing, and studied it. Uncle Dave looked comfortable, happy. His friend also comfortable, happy, and oddly familiar. Close-cropped hair, slightly bugged ears, a gap between the two front teeth.

Aunt Kris almost smashed into me, carrying down the emptied Jiffy Pop tin and two empty plastic water cups, the other three still in the carpeted loft.

"Who's that?" I asked her, pointing at the picture.

"That's Oliver North." She replied. "And your Uncle David at the White House. Oliver North is an American hero."

"Oliver North?" I repeated loud and heard music playing. "Oliver North," I whispered, almost like praying. Of course I knew he was an American hero. The Marine lieutenant colonel had crashed my young world earlier that summer with wall-to-wall news coverage of what was being called the Iran-Contra affair. That same exact close-cropped hair, slightly bugged ears, gap between the two front teeth, dressed in fancy military greens sitting behind that red table, unflinchingly telling members of congress that, unlike them, he wasn't afraid to punch godless

Communism in the mouth. That he was willing to put everything on the line, even his life, just like the mujahideen in Afghanistan. Just like Uncle Dave in Vietnam, Honduras, Nicaragua, and Afghanistan too.

The fact the two knew each other didn't surprise me much—mighty men of God very clearly attract other mighty men of God—but it did make me feel that much closer to the working levers of truth and power.

A cutout of Oliver North from *Time* magazine, hand raised while being sworn in, was carefully tacked to my pitched bedroom wall back home in Coos Bay. I didn't quite know enough about what "Contras" were to tie Uncle Dave's multiple middle-1980s trips to the jungles of Honduras and Nicaragua directly to Oliver North, and when I asked, very much later, if he was tied up in the affair, I got the same exact laugh and quick subject change that I had received when asking if he had killed anyone in Vietnam.

Not that there was any real difference between defeating Communism and sharing the Gospel in my childhood mind. The Courson family had been built on a solid foundation of West Coast Protestant Christianity, blossoming into modern evangelicalism, certainly, but also Republican politics. The two blending so thoroughly, so strongly, that I knew in my heart that Democrats were sinners and cigarette smokers.

Nana, who loved jewelry, had a charm bracelet loved by each of the grandkids, as each charm held a story. The biggest, of course, was a gold elephant, symbol of the Republican Party, and the story behind it was simple.

"We are Republicans."

Nana's grandfather had shaken hands with President Lincoln; her husband had served in the Navy, fighting for democracy under the unshaking direction of Fleet Admiral Chester Nimitz; her eldest son took it to the Soviet Union in various and sundry ways. She and Grampy had been fifth-row, special invited guests at the opening of Richard M. Nixon's Yorba Linda library, and pictures of them with various important personalities from the Ronald Reagan, George H. W. Bush, and Gerald Ford administrations were sprinkled around their home along with gilded invitations to the White House, Congressional Republican events, and prayer breakfasts.

Cousin Danny's bank robbing didn't begin with a white picket fence, or more specifically, hammering the last white post into the ground, looking around the tract housing cul-de-sac, and realizing that the wide-eyed dreams of suburban middle-class bliss were bullshit. His bank robbing began, first, when he was born a Courson, into that bigger-than-life adventure, and second, when he was born a dyed-in-the-wool Republican knowing full well that rules, all of them, were there to be toyed with. And who toys with rules better than tract housing cul-de-sac, suburban middle-class Republicans?

An irrefutable historical fact.

Warren G. Harding ran a scam so bald-faced, so bold, in selling no-bid oil contracts to his friends in return for kickbacks, that the phrase "Teapot Dome scandal" is learned by every cut-rate fifth grader in the nation. Richard Nixon, taking the oath of office for a second time a few short weeks after Cousin Danny was born, could look straight at the camera, declare "I'm not a crook," and believe it while overseeing an administration so completely outside the law that Watergate replaced Teapot Dome as the high-water mark for political nefariousness. Oliver North, hand fiercely raised, knew that he was involved in a criminal enterprise from the very beginning and dared Congress to lock him up because his truth mattered more, and his boss, Ronald Reagan, was Teflon. Nothing ever stuck.

Democrats are hacks when it comes to breaking the law. A little *Monkey Business* (Gary Hart's yacht) over here, a little "I-did-not-have-sexual-relations-with-that-woman" over there. Sexual, maybe, but not sexy. Bad, but never that bad. Rod Blagojevich naming a senator and getting caught on tape saying he was "not just going to give it up for fucking nothing." Tawdry at worst. Never shattering world governments, trouncing international treaties, exploding the status quo.

When Cousin Danny was on the lam, running from the FBI and multiple police agencies, he emailed me:

> Last night I went to a party with a girl, and no joke, I shook hands and spoke briefly with the Democratic party's primary nominee for state governor here. CNN was filming. Real low profile, Dan! Maybe I just torpedoed her entire political career! Maybe I could sell the fact that she's hanging out with a fugitive to her Republican opponent for a few bucks! This gets so fucking surreal sometimes, and yes, sorta fun. But fucking stressful, too.

You can take the boy out of the Republican Party, but you can never take the Republican Party out of the boy. Thinking about how to lay waste to Democrats, perpetually back-footed, in some new, never-before-attempted way, is exactly the same drive, same inborn ability, it requires to stand over a shaking teller, waiting for her to pile the money on the marble counter after slipping a typed note in all capitals that begins, "THIS IS A ROBBERY."

CHAPTER 3

A BRIEF HISTORY OF BANK ROBBERY IN AMERICA

Bank robbery belongs to America as much as baseball, apple pie, Tom Ford, and MTV. Sure, Ned Kelly became handsomely famous down in dirty Australia, the dashing bushman knocking off banks to support a broader insurrection. He was played by Heath Ledger on film (also starring Orlando Bloom).

Heath Ledger and Orlando Bloom? Does it get better than that? More sexy? No, but in *Stockholm*, a movie about a bank bust gone awry, we see Ethan Hawke playing the sweltering Lars Nystrom, a fictional version of the even hotter actual criminal Jan-Erik Olsson, a bank robber so beautiful that he made bound-and-gagged tellers fall in love with him, thus introducing an entirely new psychological disorder—Stockholm syndrome.

"Without weapons, hatred, or violence" was the note Frenchman Albert Spaggiari left behind after robbing a bank in Nice in 1976 by digging through the sewer, breaking into the vault, and absconding with somewhere between forty-six and one hundred million francs. He brought wine and pâté with him, for the robbery, and sat in the safe picnicking before disappearing with his massive haul. He was captured later, but escaped from a judge's office when he opened a window (he had first complained about the heat) and jumped out. He landed on a car below and was whisked away on a motorcycle. Spaggiari fled to South America. His robbery was dramatized in the film *Sans Arme, ni Haine, ni Violence*, which came out in 2008. It was called *The Easy Way* in English, and though the film starred Jean-Paul Rouve as Spaggiari, Jean-Paul, while handsome, ain't no Heath Ledger.

Others, specifically Europeans, have done it better, clearly, and history's first bank robbery is lost to time—maybe the ancient Egyptians, maybe the Aztecs, maybe some odd Roman tired of a Medici's platformed heel upon his neck who decided to pop the Florentine Medici Bank. But none of this diminishes American ownership of the crime.

The very first US heist on record occurred in Quaker Philadelphia, the City of Brotherly Love, in 1793, a mere decade after the colonies had won separation from Mother England. The story, published soon after under the title "Narrative of Patrick Lyon, Who Suffered Three Months Severe Imprisonment in Philadelphia Gaol on Merely a Vague Suspicion of Being Concerned in a Robbery of the Bank of Pennsylvania, With His Remarks Thereon" detailed an almost modern tale of derring-do.

The Bank of Pennsylvania, established in 1780 in order to help fund the colonial armies, was temporarily being housed inside Carpenters' Hall, home of the carpenters' guild. On the night of August 31, an almost unbelievable $162,281 disappeared from the vault. Suspicion immediately fell upon Patrick Lyon, a blacksmith, who had worked on the hinges and locks of Carpenters' Hall. Though Lyon swore his innocence, he was swiftly locked up.

Three months later, however, the stolen money began trickling in as deposits to the very same bank. They were flagged and the true perpetrators revealed. One, a bank porter, had slept in the bank the night of the robbery. The other, a member of the carpenters' guild, had crafted the scheme.

Their plan had been executed perfectly and would have worked, except the inside man died of yellow fever, and the carpenter, lacking savvy, began making his deposits in the same bank he had robbed. When confronted, he confessed the entire thing and was forgiven in exchange for returning all the money.

The wrongly accused Lyon would go on to become an author, penning the widely read and brilliantly titled narrative and later suing the bank for his prosecution, as they continued to pursue him as an accomplice to the crime despite no evidence. The jury awarded him an unprecedented $12,000, and he cut a deal with the bank for a kingly $9,000, or more than a decade's worth of wages. Lyon's portrait was painted by John Neagle, a very fashionable artist, and hangs in the Pennsylvania Academy of the Fine Arts to this day.

An auspicious beginning for American bank robbing with winners all around, fame and riches flowing to each involved— even the inside man who died of yellow fever but spent his last few days on earth wealthier than President Washington. This bonanza possibly set the hook for bank robbery's future image as both lucrative and victimless in this new free land that liked to believe in those things.

Less than one hundred years later, the still-young country fought a brutal Civil War that led to a devastated South and a new brand of outlaw. Missouri bushwhacker Jesse James (played by Brad Pitt in *The Assassination of Jesse James by the Coward Robert Ford*, a name only half as long as Patrick Lyon's eponymous narrative but a film twice as boring), was the most famous of the era.

James and his gang, a collection of ex-Confederate soldiers, achieved fame and some fortune by thumbing their noses at the same republic that they had lost to in that dirty Civil War. They hit bank after bank through Iowa, Texas, Kansas, and West Virginia with dramatic flair, often selecting targets that were tied to Republican politicians, sometimes wearing costumes like Ku Klux Klan hoods, sometimes putting on shows for bystanders, wagging their guns around, delivering monologues, creating an enjoyable Shakespearean spectacle.

Tales of their exploits were breathlessly recounted in secessionist-friendly newspapers, and James became a symbol of defiance against Reconstruction, or ugly guerilla rage, depending upon the reader's penchant. His bank robberies were a punch in the mouth to those who dared dictate how Southern life should be lived and who Southern farmers could own. He was eventually shot in the head, unarmed, after a string of failed robberies, by Robert Ford, a member of James's gang who had decided to collect the bounty on the famous outlaw instead of continuing the wayward life. James was straightening a painting in his home when the fatal bullet entered his brain. Strange yet poetic.

As America attempted to heal its wounds and expanded westward, into the frontier, banks popped up in order to support and provide liquidity, while charging heavy interest, to brave pioneer men and women. With these banks came opportunity.

Robert LeRoy Parker, born in Utah as one of thirteen children to British immigrant Mormon parents, and Harry Alonzo Longabaugh, who had traveled west via covered wagon with his parents and cousins, were two such opportunists. Better known as Butch Cassidy and the Sundance Kid, respectively, the two, along with their Wild Bunch, carried out a string of bank robberies throughout the new states and territories and earned such acclaim that peak Paul Newman and peak Robert Redford (at the height of his Robert Redfordness) played them in the cinematic version of their exploits, setting the bar impossibly high for Heath Ledger, Ethan Hawke, and Brad Pitt by carrying a film that won multiple Academy Awards and being remembered as two of the greatest performances ever.

Robbing banks with linen napkins from America's first chain restaurant covering their faces, flirting with tellers, hiding in caves while participating in a group love affair with gorgeous outlaw sisters Josie and Ann Bassett, running to South America when the heat got too hot with beauty Etta Place, and robbing banks in Argentina, Butch and Sundance pushed the technicolor narrative of romanticized bank robbers to the masses who couldn't help but love it. And cheer.

Both were handsome and well-mannered, thoughtful and interesting. Contemporary newspaper accounts portrayed Butch and Sundance as dashing, and the public embraced this new perception of the bank robber as a lovable rogue. These men were living, really living, and almost cuddly. Both rejected wanton violence, with Butch even bragging that he never once killed a man or woman.

According to history, the two died together under a hail of Bolivian bullets after their lodging house in the small mining town in San Vicente was given up and surrounded by soldiers, but rumors persisted that Butch had made it away. In fact, Josie Bassett insisted until her death in 1964 that Butch had visited her in 1920 after returning from South America. His sister, Lula Parker Betenson, says he visited the family in Utah in 1925 and they ate blueberry pie. She said her outlaw brother admitted, "All I done is make a wreck of my life," then moved to Washington State, where he died of pneumonia as America staggered under the weight of its Great Depression.

On October 29, 1929, after a decade of roaring good times, the stock market crashed, worldwide GDP fell by 15 percent over the next few years, and the same banks robbed by Jesse James, Butch, and Sundance locked their doors to prevent losing all that liquidity to the furious mobs gathering outside, wailing and gnashing teeth.

"Black Tuesday" changed the makeup of America, grinding a robust economy to a halt and erasing billions of dollars' worth of family savings almost overnight. Millions upon millions lost jobs, lost homes, went hungry, were pushed to the very fringes of a safety-net-free cataclysmic social failing.

Banks were instantly blamed for the disaster, as heedless speculation—fueled by the belief that the market would go up forever—had led to ill-advised lending. The whole mess affected almost all Americans, including the son of a German immigrant named Matthaias, who had come to the United States in 1851 from a region of Lorraine, then under French control.

Matthaias chose a new last name based on the town Dillingen, near where he grew up and famous for being destroyed during the Thirty Years' War and home to a white, blunt renaissance castle. Dillingen became Dillinger at Ellis Island, before Matthaias moved to the modern planned city of Indianapolis, Indiana. There, Matthaias Dillinger fathered John Wilson Dillinger, who, in turn, fathered John Herbert Dillinger, and they were all happy until John Herbert got busted for his "bewildering personality" as a preteen. John H. didn't care, continued down his wayward path, quit school and got sent to prison for stealing a car, enlisted in the Navy, deserted, then robbed a grocery store for $50 with the umpire of the semiprofessional baseball team where he played shortstop. John received a hefty ten-to-twenty-year sentence and vowed, "I will be the meanest bastard you ever saw when I get out of here."

Behind the high brick walls of Indiana's state prison, the twenty-one-year-old John Dillinger took his pledge seriously. He began learning whatever he could about the mean bastard lifestyle from fellow inmates. One, a tall, thin, soft-spoken Hoosier named Harry Pierpont, was serving time for bank robbery and taught John everything he knew about the art, giving him details, contacts on the outside, tricks, and tips. In exchange for this veritable treasure trove of knowledge, John promised to help Pierpont escape when he got out.

Two others, James Clark and Walter Dietrich, were also doing time for bank robbery as part of Herman "Baron" Lamm's gang. Lamm had served as a Prussian army officer but was drummed out for cheating at cards just before the outbreak of World War I. He emigrated to the United States and embarked upon a life of bank robbery, utilizing his military training to bring a level of straight-backed, shined-boot seriousness to the generally chaotic venture.

During a stint in a Utah prison, Lamm formalized his thinking and completely developed "The Lamm Technique," which included observing banks for days, pre-robbery, watching the movement of employees and hours when busiest, mapping the possible escape routes, having one of his men pose as a journalist to gain working knowledge of the bank's inside, and employing nondescript cars with souped-up engines driven by ex-rum runners.

After getting out of prison, Lamm set out on a next-level spree, hitting banks across the country with a never-before-witnessed efficiency. In the former Prussian officer's hands, what was once a crime of passion became a scientific, efficient exercise. Police forces were not equipped to deal with his technical superiority.

Fate intervened one night after a bank robbery in Clinton, Indiana, though. Lamm and his gang had made it to the car, a fine first step, but then saw a local townsperson coming up behind them, armed and ready. The police had organized the state's citizenry to try and even the playing field, a tough-to-account-for development. The car's driver got scared, whipped an ill-advised U-turn, and popped a tire.

The gang jumped into another car, which happened to have a governor on it to stop its elderly driver from speeding, so they jumped into another car, which was low on gas, so they jumped into another car, which overheated.

They all ended up in a cornfield, surrounded. Lamm died in the ensuing gun battle, along with seventy-one-year-old Dad Landy. James Clark and Walter Dietrich were captured and sent to prison. They brought their expertise in "The Lamm Technique" with them, and passed it on to John Dillinger, who became an expert too, forever altering bank robbery's already rich history.

Dillinger robbed his first bank days after release, his second a few months later. True to his word, he helped break Pierpont and six others out of prison by smuggling pistols into the laundry room, then went on a year-long run through the Midwest with Pierpont and other assorted derelicts that riveted the nation.

The Great Depression was at its height—picture sallow, dirt-streaked faces in breadlines, empty pockets turned inside out—and press stories of brazen men dressed in suits, driving in fast cars, wielding machine guns, sticking it to the very institutions that had caused so much pain were feasted upon by a greatly depressed public. Dillinger, a dapper figure with a devil-may-care smirk, lightly disheveled slick hair, and a pencil mustache, just screamed "Johnny Depp," and, thankfully, that is exactly who played him in Michael Mann's cinematic retelling *Public Enemies*, which was not as good as *Butch Cassidy and the Sundance Kid* but better than *The Assassination of Jesse James by the Coward Robert Ford*.

Dillinger was dashing and charismatic. Magnetic. He courted attention, hosting press conferences after getting caught and even using them to telegraph his next escape. During the robberies, he would perform for bank customers—a stage production of charisma and charm in front of cowering workaday folk—allegedly having them put away their own money while declaring, "I'm taking the bank's money, not yours."

His successes, and the attention paid, were simply too great a burden for a nation that required, at the very least, a veneer of law and order. President Herbert Hoover bolstered the mostly neutered Bureau of Investigation, changing its name to the Federal

Bureau of Investigation, and empowered its cross-dressing director, J. Edgar Hoover, to wipe "this Dillinger embarrassment" away. Hoover took his mission equally seriously, declaring John Herbert Dillinger the very first "public enemy number one." And on July 22, 1934, FBI agents tracked him to a Chicago movie theater, where he was watching Clark Gable and Myrna Loy in Manhattan Melodrama, a fun little crime caper. When the film was over, Dillinger exited and was gunned down in an adjacent alley. Onlookers rushed in and reportedly dipped handkerchiefs in his pooled blood to keep for souvenirs. John Dillinger's death was splashed across the front pages of newspapers from New York to Los Angeles, a city that had quite glamorously come into its own.

Hollywood and its studios, which had exploded in the 1920s to become America's fifth-largest industry, were at the apex of their power by the mid-1930s. Production, distribution, and exhibition were all controlled by four major players, churning out more than six hundred films a year and monopolizing the money. *Gone with the Wind, All Quiet on the Western Front, The Wizard of Oz,* and *The Philadelphia Story,* just to name a few, all came out during this time. Also *Citizen Kane,* still considered the greatest film ever made, depicting a lightly fictionalized version of William Randolph Hearst's life.

Hearst had made his name in publishing by taking his mining magnate father's stodgy newspaper, the *San Francisco Examiner,* expanding it to multiple titles, and crafting a new, flamboyant form of journalism—described as "yellow" by detractors—that pushed lurid human interest stories featuring salaciousness, sexiness, blood, bullets, and blonds. Though not directly responsible for the coverage of Jesse James, Hearst's papers made Butch and Sundance famous by writing of their exploits with grand flourishes; then they shot Dillinger to the stars, for what is bank robbery without an accompanying narrative painting the scene as a romantic thrill with bad guys, good guys, souped-up cars, chases, gunfights, hostages, and audacious plans carried out audaciously?

A master showman, Hearst knew that "Truth is not only stranger than fiction, it is more interesting." And "Putting out a newspaper without promotion is like winking at a girl in the dark—well-intentioned, but ineffective." Truth and promotion—with America's public eating up every word, swooning at every incandescent wink. And bank robbers, again, were perfect front-page material.

There had been a major demographic shift during the Great Depression, with more and more people moving to cities in order to find work. Hearst's gossip, rumor, and good times spread like wildfire through packed-in, overworked, and underfed people. These cities continued to swell during World War II, and when victorious soldiers came home after smashing Herman Lamm's hometown Germans, they decided they wanted to have enlightened children, American-made cars, single-dwelling homes, and room to stretch and grow.

The baby boom was on, and a sense of euphoric utopianism descended from sea to shining sea, but mostly the Pacific, where California, through its robust Hollywood propaganda machine, had come to represent the absolute ideal life. Sun throughout the year, swimming pools in backyards, megawatt smiles in well-stocked grocery stores.

No one was immune to the charms, including William Randolph Hearst, who pushed the California suburban ideal to its

glorious maximum, though Hearst didn't raise his five sons—
George Randolph, William Randolph Jr., John Randolph, and
twins Randolph Apperson and David Whitmire—in his enchanted
California castle hovering over the small town of San Simeon;
rather he kept them cold on the East Coast.

Randolph Apperson Hearst, born fourth and just ahead of
David, was brought up on the Atlantic, being born in New York and
attending Harvard before racing to San Francisco and fathering
five of his own children, including Patricia, a smart enough girl
who chose nearby University of California, Berkeley as part of
her gilded path.

And there she was on February 4, 1974, in her near-campus
apartment, just nineteen years old with her mustachioed fiancé,
enjoying a clear winter morning when a leftist guerilla organization burst through her door, bashed her head, tossed her in the
trunk of their car, and drove into infamy.

The Symbionese Liberation Army had been lightly known
before the brazen kidnapping, but all of a sudden it had the
nation's attention. Patty's father had not thought it necessary to
hire bodyguards for her, seeing as he did not have any controlling
interest in the Hearst organization.

She was allegedly kept in a closet for some time while being
indoctrinated with SLA pamphlets and coloring books. Her cap-
tors eventually demanded that her family give $70 of food to every
needy person in the Bay Area. The *New York Times* estimated
this would cost $203,251,000; though Randolph gave away some
$2 million worth of food, Patty was not released, and the demand
was raised to $6 million. The Hearst Corporation took over the
negotiations, and then the wheels came off, as grainy closed-
circuit television footage was released of a lithe brunette, dressed

all in black, carrying a semiautomatic M1 carbine, and, according to KRON San Francisco, "apparently aiming at between five and eight bank employees and customers who were ordered face down" behind the lemon-yellow counters of the Hibernia Bank in San Francisco's Outer Sunset district.

According to contemporary news reports, "Witnesses say as bank robberies go, this one was extremely well planned," but, in truth, and with the searing klieg light of hindsight, it seemed a bit of a mess. The five-member crew lingered in the bank for longer than five minutes, shot two men who entered the bank after the robbery was in progress, managed to hustle just over $10,000, and almost left Patty Hearst behind (eyewitnesses reported her running after the getaway vehicle).

Days later, the SLA released an audio message where Patty's own subdued voice declared, "Greetings to the people. This is Tania. On April 15, my comrades and I expropriated $10,660.02 from the Sunset branch of Hibernia bank. Casualties could have been avoided had the persons involved kept out of the way and cooperated with the people's forces until after our departure."

The entire story was a journalist's dream, yellowing itself without need for flourish or plume. Kidnapped heiress, leftist guerrilla group, bank robbery, escape, manifestos, seven-headed serpent logo, etc. One that William Randolph himself could not have conjured, but that was also his genius. Truth stranger than fiction *and* more interesting.

Patty was captured months later, after a bizarre shootout, and said that she had been brainwashed. She was still found guilty and sentenced to seven years' hard time. After serving two, president Jimmy Carter commuted her sentence, and she started acting, starring across from pre–John Dillinger Johnny Depp in

John Waters's *Cry-Baby*. Natasha Richardson played Patty in the cinematic retelling *Patty Hearst: Her Own Story*.

Brainwashed or not, her confession tape contains the realest of truths. Namely, departure, as it relates to bank robbery, is the key. The SLA screwed up by killing on the way out, and it caught up with them all. Jesse James would flee in purposefully circuitous routes, Butch and Sundance would plant fresh horses along their way, Herman Lamm juiced his getaway cars, taping maps to their dashboards and doing trial runs in different weather conditions, John Dillinger juiced his cars even more—and the SLA operated in California, a place where multiple freeways and wide boulevards created a dream scenario, allowing them to initially get away even after a severe mistake.

In his book *Norco '80*, about an audacious hit in the shadow of the San Gabriel mountains involving severe damage to thirty police cars and one police helicopter due to gunfire during a wild pursuit, author Peter Houlahan wrote that from 1985 to 1995, 3,500 bank branches in greater Los Angeles were hit 17,106 times. In 1992, the peak of that decade, there were a difficult-to-comprehend 2,641 heists—that's one every forty-five minutes of each banking day.

An even more cinematic robbery, and attempted getaway, unfolded live on television on the morning of February 28, 1997, just five years after the peak. Romanian-born Emil Matasareanu and his partner, Larry Phillips Jr., known as the High Incident Bandits for their previous over-the-top hits, entered Bank of America's North Hollywood branch dressed all in black, with homemade body armor protecting their vital organs, an arsenal of modified semiautomatic weapons, and watches sewn into their black gloves, timers set for eight minutes.

The two had met at a gym in Venice Beach, California, almost a decade earlier, bonded over their love of bodybuilding and high-powered weaponry, and started robbing armored cars and banks before getting pulled over, in Glendale, California, with an illegal arsenal in their car. The law was unaware of the previous robberies and only arrested them on charges of speeding and possession of unregistered weapons. Each served one hundred days in prison, got out, and began meticulously planning another job.

Past experience had taught them they could overwhelm guards, tellers, bank managers, any other security with sheer ridiculous force, so they redoubled their weapons cache, cased a bank in North Hollywood, listened to scanners to sort average police responses in the area, and figured if they were in and out in eight minutes all would be fine.

Things went wrong almost immediately, when patrol officers spotted a suspicious duo wearing all black entering the bank, thereby negating the planned-for eight minutes. The bank schedule had changed, and the vault was not even full. Even if it had been full, the branch manager no longer had access to it, according to new guidelines. Still, with all hell breaking loose, workaday citizens were still trying to bank.

When the pair strolled outside with a depressingly low amount of money, soiled because a dye pack had already gone off, the High Incident Bandits were met by police with guns drawn.

Over the next forty-four minutes, Matasareanu and Phillips exchanged more than two thousand rounds of ammunition with a severely under-gunned LAPD, moving slowly down North Hollywood's Laurel Canyon Boulevard while news helicopters swirled overhead, capturing every thump of every bullet leaving its chamber.

Detective Thomas Culotta, on scene that fateful day, told the *Los Angeles Times*, "I saw my rounds hit his black jacket, and as I shot at him, he kept coming. Was this a dream? I wasn't sure, but as this specter made eye contact with me, he pointed his weapon and fired right at me. . . . I remember asking God, 'Is this the day?' Death was coming."

Death did eventually come for the two bank robbers. Matasareanu and Phillips ended their beautiful friendship a few blocks from each other. Phillips went first, getting pinned down by gunfire and taking his own life. Matasareanu, who was hit multiple times in the legs, bled out before paramedics arrived. Somehow, no officers or civilians died, though twelve officers and eight civilians were injured.

Bank robbery numbers dropped precipitously after the North Hollywood spectacle, when banks attempted to "harden up" by employing security guards, utilizing bulletproof glass, and changing floorplans. Police were issued better equipment (including automatic weapons), branch managers all lost access to vaults, and mandatory sentencing laws were put in place in order to discourage the practice.

In 2006, almost a decade after the North Hollywood shootout and the year Cousin Danny robbed his first bank, the FBI reports in its crime statistics that there were 7,272 total violations of the Federal Bank Robbery and Incidental Crimes statute. The vast majority were commercial banks, with armored cars, savings and loan associations, mutual savings banks, and credit unions accounting for less than 10 percent. More than $70 million, in cash, was lifted from these institutions, with a further $2 million in checks—and zero dollars in food stamps.

Only $9 million was recovered.

Nine thousand people were determined to have been involved in the robberies, the overwhelming majority male, either white or black, and 39 percent were identified after the fact, leaving 61 percent free and clear. Of those taken into custody, 46 percent were "determined to be users of narcotics" and 22 percent had been busted for bank robbery previously.

A note, slid to the teller, was employed more than half the time, a firearm less than a third. The poor teller was also the only target in 6,832 of the 7,272 robberies. Only 395 brave souls dared attempt the vault; ten were bold enough to head for the safe-deposit area. A total of eighty hostages were taken over the year, forty-nine of them bank employees. There were 129 injuries, the vast majority bank employees, and thirteen deaths, just ten of them the bank robber himself.

The West is, regionally, the most common place banks get robbed, and California is its clear champion. The Golden State saw 915 bank robberies in 2006. That's more than New York, New Jersey, Pennsylvania, and Connecticut combined. Texas, coming in second, had a mere 394.

California. The mixture of suburbs extending over the horizon, standalone suburban banks meant to provide a sense of casual family-friendly ease, gorgeously paved wide roads that lead to massive freeways—multiple massive freeways that lead to other massive freeways, large boulevards, or other different suburbs—tens, possibly even hundreds of miles away created the ideal milieu for robbing banks, then getting away. The optimal set, padding the over-60-percent success rate.

"Bank robbery is all about the getaway," Cousin Danny told me years later, while on a protracted getaway from the FBI. "Everything else is incidental. On my way out of one robbery, a guy in the parking lot decided to jump in his car and follow me. I had parked across the street, so by the time I sprinted to my car and jumped in, he was pulling up behind me.

"I punched it, and he followed me. I think he was in a truck—can't quite remember—but not too close, and I could see him on his cell, in my rearview. After a bunch of quick turns on surface streets, I pulled into a dirt construction lot, floored it, and spun the wheel. I remember a cloud of dust, full-on drifting, and drove my truck straight at him, a game of chicken. He swerved off, I rocketed past, and by the time he turned around I was far enough away to lose him.

"It was gnarly. The news reports later had a description of my truck. I had no plates on it, so I know he talked with the cops about it. I'll never forget that moment racing toward his truck, looking at each other for a split second, just fucking focused on getting away no matter what."

It takes two things to make a great bank robbery, though—or maybe three. The getaway, sure. The desperation or guts to attempt one, yes. But also, and maybe most important, a yellow journalist there on the backside needing to tell the tale in all its lurid glory with exactly the same ill-wrought conviction the bank robber has to rob a bank.

The names Ned Kelly, Kaj Hansson, Albert Spaggiari, Jesse James, Butch and Sundance, Herman Lamm, John Dillinger, Patty Hearst, and a whole panoply of others would be meaningless if it weren't for the tireless work of journalists bringing their stories to life. Even better, yellow journalists who knew how to twist and tug a true story into proper entertainment, blending fact with fabulous. Even better, a surf journalist so yellowed, his trash prose so odious, that the great Kelly Slater had blocked him across all social media channels. Whose own mother had to apologize to her brother, my Uncle Dave, for raising a more corrupt son than his, who happened to be my serially bank-robbing Cousin Danny.

It takes me.

She last communicated via my father's Hotmail account, declaring she would have to apologize to her brother, my Uncle Dave, Cousin Danny's father, because she had raised a more corrupt, odious, harmful, and hurtful son than his own serial bank robber, fugitive, and art thief. A tough pill to swallow, but Cousin Danny needs my journalistic dirty. History, if it has proven anything at all, has proved this.

CHAPTER 4

JESUS FREAKS

But oh boy, our Nana certainly would have grabbed both our triceps with her immaculately manicured fingers, adorned with chunky gold rings, and twisted to excruciating pain in the way she was most famous for if she was standing between Cousin Danny and me right now.

The Coursons were ruled by that twist. Nana's four children—Uncle Dave, my mother, Uncle Jonny, Uncle Jimmy—and all of her grandchildren felt that twist, some more sternly than others. That twist *hurt*. She loved that it hurt, as she was a small woman and always immaculately manicured—not the typical look for a sadist—and the surprised "ouch!" from the mouth of the person whose tricep was being twisted brought her much joy.

Nana, Mary Elizabeth Stine, was born in 1927, the same year the first transatlantic telephone call was made, the same year the first Volvo rolled off the production line in Gothenburg, Sweden. She was proud of her entire name but particularly the "Stine" bit, which she insisted, later in life, to be a bastardization of Stein, since her dream-of-all-dreams was to be a Jewish grandmother living in Israel. She was, instead, from the British Isles with a hefty bit of German Pentecostal and grew up in prewar Southern California.

Her father was a hardworking plastering contractor who had been the captain of the track team at the University of Southern California. Her mother, from rural Washington State, became homecoming queen and won a scholarship to Oregon State by bicycling newspaper subscriptions to neighboring logging camps. The two met at a chaste dinner party, were married soon after, and raised their family in La Crescenta, a small town just north and east of Los Angeles, the name of which had been bastardized from the Spanish *el creciente* by an early settler named Benjamin B. Briggs.

During the Great Depression, Nana had gotten sick during a diphtheria outbreak, and the doctor, unfortunately named Dr. Craven, pronounced her dead and pulled a blanket over her three-year-old head. But Nana's mother refused to believe and called in the pastor and elders from her church, who did the brave work Dr. Craven couldn't, praying her back to life.

Each Sunday would include two long church services, one in the morning and one at night, interrupted by a pot roast Sunday lunch, but if they were really in luck, a big-tent Pentecostal revival would be rolling through town, and then it would be days upon endless days of fun.

Pentecostalism, drawing its name from the Greek word for "fiftieth" and referring to the day that Jesus's disciples received the Holy Spirit, is a vibrant, bright, full-throated expression of Christianity. Faith healing, speaking in tongues, pastors marching around on wooden stages striking fear into hearts with vivid descriptions of hell's fire and brimstone where all sinners would cook for eternity. The movement didn't have a single founder, but many different theologians, evangelists, pastors, and preachers—white, black, male, female—feeding one ethos: a radical evangelicalism. A charismatic, physically experienced, all-encompassing faith.

Nana loved every bit of it, both church and revival. The sounds, smells, songs sung at maximum volume, the altar call at the end where the unsaved would come up front, kneel down, ask Jesus to come into their hearts and, by God's grace, dodge that fire and brimstone.

She described her childhood and teenage years as filled with joy but also filled with rules. "You see, in the precious Pentecostal church around which our lives revolved, there were to be no movies, no makeup, no card-playing, no bowling, no dancing, no going to skating rinks, no short hair, no permanents, no hair coloring, no slacks for women, no mixed-sex swimming, no going to pool halls, and no going to pizza parlors—not to mention no smoking, swearing, or drinking."

Or bank robbing, I think, but certainly not yellow surf journalism that mixes mixed-sex swimming, smoking, swearing, and drinking with cocaine. Cousin Danny and I both would have gotten the worst triceps twists ever and would have seriously deserved them.

We weren't raised this way. Weren't raised to "kick against the goads," that gorgeously poetic Biblical phrase meaning "ruinous resistance." Nana never ruinously resisted. She married Grampy, a handsome Navy man on leave who swept her off her feet by coming to her cousin's house one fated afternoon between the morning and evening church services and playing the trumpet.

After Grampy returned from the Pacific theater at the end of World War II, the two of them moved from La Crescenta to Seattle to enroll at the Northwest Bible Institute (now Northwest Bible College) so they could train to become missionaries. As it works, Grampy's meager G.I. Bill only went so far, and between classes he was soon out looking for work, dropping his résumé off everywhere.

One afternoon, as he was pounding the pavement, Seattle's sky opened up and, once again, drenched the already saturated earth below. Grampy slipped underneath the first awning he could find, which happened to belong to a bank, and decided to drop his résumé off there too. He was hired on the spot and spent the next forty-six years climbing the corporate ladder before eventually becoming, ironically in hindsight, a bank president.

Nana was disappointed, initially, not to be a missionary, but she trusted God. Then she mothered four children who would each go to Bible school and become either legendary missionaries or legendary pastors.

Uncle Dave was first, born in Seattle, followed by my mother just two years later, in Vancouver, Washington, as Grampy jumped banks. Then Uncle Jonny three years later, after a hop to Campbell, California, just outside San Jose, rounded out by Uncle Jimmy five years after that, also in Campbell, to end it all. Children in Bible college, high school, junior high, and kindergarten and still no ruinous resistance anywhere—just church parties, church friends, church services, and prayer breakfasts. Everyone going along, getting along in a 1950s, 1960s earthly American paradise.

There were only the slightest of bumps along the freshly cooled pavement. Like when Sally Cool, a leather-jacket-wearing, rock-'n'-roll-listening, black-dyed-hair cousin who needed straightening out came to stay with the Coursons in Campbell. Sally's mother, Nana's younger sister, had married a nice Christian boy named Tim Cool, and their lives were typically sublime and wholesome until Tim kicked against the goads, married other women on the side, started dabbling in the criminal life, joined the just-founded Hells Angels Motorcycle Club in Fontana, California, and caused all sorts of mayhem.

One day, when Tim was driving Nana's sister home, his car suddenly swerved to the curb and came to a stop. Nana's sister thought her derelict husband was playing some sort of bad joke, but no, he had instead died instantly due to complications from a metal plate in his head installed after an earlier motorcycle accident.

Sally Cool, the daughter of Tim and Nana's sister, needed straightening out, and Nana straightened her out no problem

And then there was Uncle Dave. He'd enrolled in Biola University, originally the Bible Institute of Los Angeles, in Southern California directly after graduating from high school. It was a Christian college founded by the very same Pentecostals that thrilled young Nana, now teaching the "fundamentals" of the faith. The Coursons had, themselves, moved from Assemblies of God, the world's largest Pentecostal denomination, to the Baptist church, far more doctrinally concerned and generally conservative.

Uncle Dave was restless at Biola and struggled with his grades because he had adventure in his blood, and while dispensationalism, substitutionary atonement, and the historical-grammatical method were edifying, they were not necessarily adrenalized. So one perfectly temperate day, he decided to enlist in the Marine Corps, guaranteeing himself frontline action.

It was the early 1960s, and Vietnam was getting hotter by the minute. Even though Nana and Grampy were as staunchly patriotic as ever, Republican to the very bone, eager to stop the toppling of dominos by godless commies, having their firstborn son volunteer to fly halfway around the world and drop into a dicey conflict as a Marine gunnery sergeant was not entirely welcome. Still, Uncle Dave straightened out, came home after his tours of duty, planted a church with his younger brother Uncle Jonny, and then founded Christian Emergency Relief Teams, becoming the missionary that Nana and Grampy once dreamed of being with a staunchly patriotic, Republican-to-the-very-bone flavor.

My mother made a quick mistake by not following Uncle Dave to Biola, opting instead to head north to Seattle Pacific College (now Seattle Pacific University), a Free Methodist school in North Queen Anne. Even though she had been born in Vancouver, Washington, California had shaped her formative years, and the perpetually gray, cold, windy Pacific Northwest drove her to depression.

She did meet my father, a very popular cheerleader, or "cheer king," from nearby Kent who was also attending Seattle Pacific, but fled south midway through her sophomore year to the now-abandoned-by-Uncle-Dave Biola and loved, absolutely loved, every second of her time there. All of the wonderful discussions sussing out premillennialism as superior to postmillennialism. Each of the spirited debates on the inerrancy of scripture, to say nothing of the various liberal arts courses she loved. And there she flowered, capturing the zeitgeist of modern fundamentalist evangelicalism with that fiery red hair cut into a chic flip, the very image of mid-1960s Kingston Trio cleanliness with a touch of Peter, Paul and Mary thrown in for flair.

Her yearbooks from those years are pure saturated-color photo promise. Biola had recently moved from downtown Los Angeles to an Orange County–adjacent suburb called La Mirada. The campus reflected the surroundings: clean, fresh, new. Warm California sun bathing every last inch. Her girlfriends looked bubbly and cute in their mid-thigh skirts. Male friends too, with hair slightly longer than their fundamentalist fathers but wearing the same black, thick-framed glasses. Smiles everywhere, unburdened by the now-clear disaster in Vietnam, racial discord closer to home, drugs chewing through cities, riots on non-Christian college campuses, the Beatles or the Rolling Stones.

The whole mélange was good enough to convince her younger brother, Uncle Jonny, to swing on down too, except he, like Uncle Dave, was not completely won over. The Old Testament history and New Testament history classes were fine enough— great, even—but the sociology courses and various introductions to English literature that so thrilled my mother didn't grab Uncle Jonny so.

The Word. Uncle Jonny only had time for the Word of God, clutching a well-worn, brown leather King James Bible and taking it with him everywhere, on every chaste date with bubbly and cute girlfriends in their mid-thigh skirts, to various introductions to English literature, to the cafeteria, called the "cafe" for short but pronounced like "caf," where students bowed heads and prayed over each meal.

He had been destined for pastoral greatness since he was three years old, sitting in the back row of San Jose's Assemblies of God church, listening to Pastor Kermit Jeffries preach that Satan knows his time is short—he has a stopwatch down to its last seconds and he's determined to grab every man and woman, every girl and boy, and drag them into the lake of fire. The message launched young Uncle Jonny off the pew, down the aisle, and into salvation.

He had a gift for preaching himself and, as a sixteen-year-old, delivered a sermon at the San Jose Rescue Mission, which served the area's homeless. He recalled, "Our youth pastor had asked me to take that service, but I had never been to a rescue mission service before. Put a suit and tie on, and I gave this message . . . on Zacchaeus, the wee little man in the tree, and I talked about the eschatological significance of Zacchaeus being not in a fig tree, which is representative of Israel, but a sycamore tree, and what it meant that Jesus called him out of a sycamore instead of a fig. I went into this whole prophecy/eschatological thing. I had twenty-two pages of text that my sister had typed, and I got to page three in my suit and tie reading and preaching and a guy in the back stood up and said, 'Would you sit down, you giant tomato!' They were hungry and just wanted to eat. I went on for another two hours. Ha!"

Redheaded Uncle Jonny loved the Word of God. In his reasoning at the time, we only have so many hours in each day, so why waste any of them reading, studying, pondering anything other than that Word of God? Biola had been founded as a bulwark against the popular early-twentieth-century movements around Christian liberalism that sought to understand the Bible in a human context, filled with errors and historical misunderstandings as opposed to divinely inspired, infallible, and perfect. The apparent issues or contradictions of the Bible were but a symptom of our failed humanity, as opposed to problems with the text.

He studied it all—the eschatology, the nuanced commentary, Hebrew and Greek subtleties. He poured himself into the

Word every waking moment. Now, it is one thing to believe but quite another to *believe*, and Uncle Jonny *believed*. Believed fiercely, comprehensively, without shade or color. Believed even more than the good, clean believing Christian coeds around him, so he began spending every off hour in neighboring churches until, one fateful Sunday morning, he rolled his 1964 Ford Econoline van down Beach Boulevard then hung a left on Talbert Avenue, which becomes MacArthur, a quick right on Fairview, and into the parking lot of a small Costa Mesa church called Calvary Chapel.

Through the nondescript wooden doors, into the nondescript sanctuary, the light buzz of traffic cruising effortlessly down wide Fairview Street heading north-south and the wider MacArthur Boulevard heading east-west. The 405 and 55 freeways intersect nearby and flow into the 5, 57, 91, 133 and the rest of the western United States.

Perfect bank robbing territory. It would be exploited regularly and, a handful of decades later, wildly exploited by a tall, skinny man wearing a nondescript hooded sweatshirt, boonie hat, and cheap, wraparound sunglasses from 7-Eleven whom the local press would dub "the Floppy Hat Bandit," my Cousin Danny, who hit a fantastic number of banks in the vicinity systematically and ruthlessly (or ruthlessly-adjacent) with a realistic-looking Glock pellet gun.

Thirty years earlier, though, the Orange County intersection was also the very beating heart of a new movement tying Nana's Pentecostal tent revivals directly to Patty Hearst–esque hippies hoping to destabilize the world.

Jesus People.

Jesus Freaks.

Disillusioned longhairs who had gone to Woodstock and/or heard about Woodstock, listened to Abbie Hoffman rant and rave, then watched Tim Cool's Hells Angels mow down their longhaired brethren at Altamont, witnessing the nasty erosion of a still-just-budding, beautiful dream.

Human selfishness, human failings, all-too-human crumbling.

The magnetic wave of a utopic counterculture, children baby boomed from the Army and Navy men returning to their Rosie the Riveter wives. Suburbia. Postwar architects who would later become famous for "tract homes" and "mid-century modern" also designing suburban roads that led straight to fabulous cloverleaf freeway entrances that led straight to the rest of the western United States had crested then crashed into an ugly haze.

Charles Manson, Symbionese Liberation Army, Patty Hearst.

Hippies once in thrall to Timothy Leary, now depressed, looked further back in time and deeper, to ancient religious traditions that had stood the test of time. Some, like David Bowie, landed on Buddhism; some, like John, Paul, and George, on Hinduism; but the lucky wound their way back to the original hippie Jesus of Nazareth and became, themselves, Jesus People or Jesus Freaks.

The values of the New Testament, when removed from the stodgy, stuffy, button-downed churches of the 1950s, resonated with lost hippies. They saw longhairs, like them, in Jesus and his ragtag band of sandal-wearing followers. How they interacted, wandered around the countryside, ate communally, shared everything, kicked against the establishment and were despised by that establishment.

They felt the actual good news in the gospel, that all are welcome in the Kingdom of God, that our greatest good is to love God and love our neighbors. That the first are last and the last are first, and that it is the peacemakers who are the children of God, not Washington, DC, warmongers.

Jesus was a superstar, a radical—he was not their parents' dullard and not held in their parents' lame churches—and so they brought him out into the streets and parks, especially in the heart of hippiedom San Francisco.

There, counterculture couple Ted and Elizabeth Wise lived in a beat commune, their marriage a drug-filled, sometimes violent, disaster. Elizabeth, tired of the mess, had grown up as a Christian and started attending a local Baptist church. Her husband followed, found the peace he was searching for, and gave his life to Jesus.

The two wanted to serve the Lord but not in the confines of a "church," which carried all the weight and stigma of a bummer patriarchy, and so opened an erstwhile symbol of the beat experience, a coffeehouse called the Living Room right in Haight-Ashbury. Hippies could be comfortable, wearing the clothes they wore, speaking the slang they spoke, listening to the music they loved now infused with Jesus's message and experiencing the love for which they had been hunting.

Protestant Christianity, broadly, had mixed feelings about the new movement, with many refusing to imagine Jesus as a dirty peacenik. Gordon Lindsay, a popular revivalist preacher and author, spoke heavily against the freaks, warning anyone who would listen that "We should not leave the scriptures and the Bible and the gospel of salvation and start down the street with protestors and the revolutionaries."

Billy Graham, on the other hand, wildly more popular than Lindsay, embraced the sea change, writing *The Jesus Generation* as a full endorsement in 1971. The book went on to become an international bestseller, attracting even more Jesus People, spreading across the nation, down to Orange County, into Calvary Chapel. Jesus Freaks like Lonnie Frisbee, the long-hair, long-beard, bellbottom-wearing young evangelist who captivated a wider and wider audience and who would pack that Calvary Chapel, then spill out into tents erected in the parking lots or nearby parks.

Lonnie Frisbee had a way with the audience—his charismatic persona, his personal story, or testimony, of a very rough life that brought him to salvation. Except it wasn't Lonnie that got Uncle Jonny's attention or why he was there. Uncle Jonny had started attending Calvary Chapel just before these hippies had poured through the door, and initially, internally, he revolted against them. "I was an Assembly of God little kid, then a Baptist elementary school, junior high, high school kid," he said. "Knew the Bible pretty well, was in church all the time, loved the Lord, really did, but something was happening, a revival was taking place with a group of people that nobody in our group, church group, thought could ever be saved.

"These dirty hippies who were doing drugs—and they had really long hair, and they didn't dress right, and they played guitars when they sang songs. This group was swept in by the grace of God, by the love of God, but in '68, '69, '70, the country was divided every bit as much as it is these days. Watts and Chicago were going up in smoke, in fire; there were riots in the streets; college kids were being shot by the National Guard at Kent State; civil rights activist Martin Luther King Jr. was gunned down; Bobby

Kennedy was gunned down; John Kennedy killed even before that. Strong feelings—all of us had strong feelings, about one side or the other. I had put a bumper sticker, as a sixteen-year-old [in '66 or '67], on the back of my 1961 Ford Falcon that read AMERICA: LOVE IT OR LEAVE IT. My brother was in Vietnam at that time, and, believe me, I was very conservative, politically—very strong in my stances—but I was seeing, in this little church I began to attend, these people that were . . . a whole different thing. They talked about Jesus and not about doctrines or about politics or 'You should be . . .' or 'Why aren't you . . .' It was just, really, love. For that to happen? It was not something you just talked yourself into or psyched yourself up for. It was a reintroduction to love.

"I went to Calvary Chapel for a couple of years, resisted all of this for a couple years, because I was at Biola, a good school, but at that time very Baptist, and this idea of having an experience with the Holy Spirit, having Him touch you and fill you, praising Him with your heart in unknown tongues and all of that was considered to be counterfeit and dangerous. As a sixteen-year-old, I gave Bible studies in youth camps about why speaking in tongues is of the devil, and boy, do I regret that. [I] had an experience at Calvary Chapel at twenty, thinking 'Whatever is going on here, I'm still a church kind of person too much and not a Jesus person enough.'"

Yes, the hippies, the Jesus Freaks, changed Uncle Jonny's entire life, but he was there, initially, because of Calvary Chapel's pastor, a buttoned-down, late-middle-age blue-collar humble man named Charles Ward Smith, or simply Pastor Chuck to the faithful.

Pastor Chuck had been born in Ventura, California, in 1927, the same year as Nana, and attended Aimee Semple McPherson's

LIFE Bible College, then next door to the Angelus Temple in Echo Park, Los Angeles.

Aimee Semple McPherson had been Nana's icon too, the biggest star in her entire universe. A female Pentecostal evangelist, McPherson achieved wild celebrity with her energetic preaching style, groundbreaking use of the radio, flamboyant stage productions including dressing as a police officer and racing a motorcycle around, a possibly staged kidnapping, and fantastic good looks, preaching dynamically while, when not on motorcycle or horse, sitting in a lacquered white art deco throne.

McPherson was wined and dined, or at least dined, by the Kennedys, Vanderbilts, and Rockefellers. She appeared in all the tabloids, founded the evangelical Foursquare movement— "Foursquare" referencing the Gospel facing every direction—and presided over the world's first megachurch under the largest domed roof in North America at the time, after receiving a vision from God about a "little home in Los Angeles."

She married three times and divorced twice—almost unheard of in early twentieth-century America, and certainly unheard of in good Christian circles. Her death, too early at the age of forty-four due to what was ruled an accidental drug overdose—also unheard of!—shocked the world. Movie stars, business tycoons, and politicians joined the 45,000 strong who lined up for hours to pay their final respects.

Pastor Chuck didn't have the natural charisma of Aimee Semple McPherson, but he did have the drive, the vision, and the ability to sense the times shifting under his feet, unlike many of his contemporaries. Pastor Chuck did not fear generational shockwaves. Donald E. Miller, professor of religion at the University of Southern California, described the man as, "Theologically conservative but simultaneously culturally avant-garde"—as unheard of as McPherson's divorces and drugs. Fittingly, it was Pastor Chuck who discovered Lonnie Frisbee, when he asked his daughter's ex–drug addict boyfriend to go and find him a hippie.

Frisbee, no relation to the flying disc, previously a self-described "nudist vegetarian," happened to be hitchhiking through his hometown, fresh from an LSD-inspired desert vision outside Palm Springs of "a vast sea of people crying out to the Lord for salvation" (David Ware Stowe, *No Sympathy for the Devil* [Chapel Hill: University of North Carolina Press, 2011], 24) with himself in front preaching the gospel. He had converted to Christianity in San Francisco, attended the Wises' coffeehouse/commune church on Haight-Ashbury, then set off south with his new bride to find his way.

Pastor Chuck was immediately struck by Frisbee's magnetism, and quickly put him in charge of a drug rehab facility associated with Calvary Chapel, then put him in charge of the Wednesday night Bible study. Soon that became so popular the little church could no longer hold the masses.

Frisbee would walk Orange County's beaches in the day, preaching the gospel to people, then bring them to church in the evenings. On the weekend, thousands would flock to Laguna Beach's Pirate Cove to be baptized by Pastor Chuck as Lonnie led worship. An unwashed, flowers-in-hair, bell-bottomed mass.

There were still grumblings from the likes of Gordon Lindsay and others who felt the gospel Frisbee and his cohorts preached didn't have any doctrinal grounding, that they were in danger of wandering into heterodoxy, or straight-up blasphemy, if not careful. None of them had been to Bible school. Many of them had taken copious amounts of LSD.

Pastor Chuck was not concerned, though, and simply began preaching through the Bible verse by verse, chapter by chapter. It was a novel approach, and exactly what Uncle Jonny had been searching for. Lonnie Frisbee, the energy of a burgeoning movement, and thousands upon thousands coming to salvation every day was thrilling, but it was fidelity to the Word, and preaching it simply, that snagged Uncle Jonny entirely. He was so taken that he began sleeping in Calvary Chapel's bathroom at night so as not to miss one moment.

Pastor Chuck, his voice loud and slow, his eyes crinkling as he smiled widely, would exposit as he traipsed linearly through the Bible. Sharing small insights from the Biblical Greek and Hebrew, pulling modern application from ancient texts. Even the "boring" verses were thoroughly dealt with, the so-and-so begat so-and-so and such-and-such begat such-and-such. Every jot and tittle was discussed, because who are we, mere humans, to pick and choose which bits of the Word of God matter?

Uncle Jonny had found his home and spent more, more, and more time at Calvary Chapel. Pastor Chuck soon recognized his dedication and his own oratorical abilities and took Uncle Jonny under his wing, mentoring him alongside a tight crew of future pastors who would go on to plant more than one thousand Calvary Chapels across the world. Uncle Jonny went back near home, to San Jose, to plant his, with his ex-Marine gunnery sergeant older brother, Uncle Dave.

I remember as a wide-eyed child hearing, in passing, mentions of their church and that it somehow hadn't worked. *But what could make that all-star combination not work?* I wondered. *Two epic brothers in service of the Lord? One an ex-Marine gunnery sergeant?* I was yet to be clued in to the sticky troubles of family and ministry or family and business or family in general, completely unaware that my ministerial family kept cards righteously close to the chest even in the best of times. I also, naïvely, didn't factor divine will into the equation.

In the mists of his church's demise, Uncle Dave shot south, founded Christian Emergency Relief Teams in Carlsbad, and became friends with Ollie North. Uncle Jonny, conversely, went north to a tiny unincorporated bit of farmland thirty-odd miles outside of Medford, Oregon.

There, he preached to the hippies who lived in the trees—the dirty hippies he once reviled who had fled San Francisco in search of a more pure, more pastoral form of life—before founding Applegate in a quaint home before eventually moving to an old ex–auto parts store off an old country road. It didn't take long before attendance burst through the seams, exactly like it had in Costa Mesa. Uncle Jonny had the charisma of Lonnie Frisbee and the fidelity of Chuck Smith. He was the perfect synthesis and, in him and a small knot of other Calvary preachers, the memory of the Jesus Movement was able to establish itself, neither burning out nor fading away. A bigger sanctuary was soon built alongside a giant outdoor amphitheater that would hold the tens of thousands of weekly worshipers.

Uncle Dave was my hero, but Uncle Jonny was the most famous person I'd ever met. Maybe the most famous person in the whole wide world, or at least my whole wide world.

CHAPTER 5

AN EVANGELICAL CAMELOT

Cousin Petey, Uncle Jonny's oldest, and I were sitting shoulder to shoulder in the backseat of Uncle Jonny's Vanagon, arguing about whether I was as much of a "Courson" as he was, only taking breaks from the serious polemic to smash our sisters, his Jessie and Christy, mine Emily, against the sliding door around each bend. He and I had been born exactly one week apart in the same San Jose hospital, the entire burgeoning Courson clan home from Vietnam and Biola, driving roots into Silicon Valley's fertile, though lightly polluted, soil. All the Courson children, save Uncle Jimmy who was just entering high school, were beginning families of their own, starting churches together, basking in the warm glow of a proud Nana ruling over it all, establishing her own West Coast Republican, profoundly Christian, cleaner and therefore better, version of John F. and Jackie's Camelot.

"You are a Courson, but not as much because your last name is Smith, so . . ." Cousin Petey repeated with a slight shrug when we hit the next straightaway.

"My mom is as much Nana and Grampy's child as your dad is," I responded through gritted teeth. "Plus, we are twelfth-cousins to Queen Elizabeth II, and you're not." My cheer king father had told me that once, and I didn't know how he knew, but also imagined it meant I was in line for the throne someday.

"Grampy," Cousin Petey chuckled. All the cousins, except the Smiths, called our grandpa "Papa," but that's what we Smiths called our dad, so after auditioning "Truck" (since he carried us around on his back), we settled on "Grampy." An unfortunate offering, in retrospect, and not helping my argument.

"But also it's just true that we are more Courson than you are. You are a Smith, and that's okay too, but . . ." And the "but" was pregnant with the truth. His father was famous. His father had really and truly put the Courson name on the map.

Pastor Jon. Pastor Jon Courson.

Nana had been saddened when her San Jose kingdom was broken up all too soon, almost directly after Petey and I came screaming into it. Uncle Dave had headed south to North County, San Diego; Uncle Jonny had gone north to southern Oregon. Grampy got a bank president job in Oregon too, four long, curvy hours north and west of Uncle Jonny and his family. My mother dragged my father to Coos Bay near Grampy, but my mom and Uncle Jonny still made a solid effort to see each other regularly, despite those four long, curvy hours, and so Petey was one of my best friends even though he semi-lorded his clear Courson superiority over me.

"Kids, would you like to see how famous I am?" Uncle Jonny turned around suddenly, with a mischievous grin spreading across his red-bearded face, a twinkle in his eye, as if he heard us and wanted to shame me completely.

"Yes!" everyone shouted, especially me. The sun had set an hour ago, and a dark gray comforter had been laid over the sky—the thick cloud layer that kept moonlight, starlight, and sunlight from reaching southern Oregon for most of the autumn, winter, and spring.

We had been taken to pizza in nearby Medford; southern Oregon's largest town claimed nearly eighty thousand residents, which put my Coos Bay's fourteen thousand to absolute shame, though it was another argument Cousin Petey and I would regularly have. Fighting tooth and nail over which nothing hometown carried more value, more general importance in the various schemes of things. He would claim population, proximity to California, the fact that Medford had a real mall. I would claim that Coos Bay once provided more woodchips to China than any other American city and also had a real mall, but he insisted Pony Village didn't count because it was in neighboring North Bend and also tiny, with the only "name-brand" store being a Bon Marché.

"Okay . . ." Uncle Jonny said, puncturing the din. "Now, watch the hill up in front of us . . ." while flipping the Vanagon's headlights to bright. I stared, completely blown away, as the road winding its way down began to light up like a Christmas tree. One car after another flipping their headlights to bright in response.

In reality, it was a standard reply to a rude driver. Uncle Jonny, like Chuck Smith before him, was ridiculously humble and simply sharing a funny trick. In my childhood mind, though, it was further proof that Uncle Jonny, *my* Uncle Jonny, was wildly famous, fans recognizing his vehicle even under that dark gray comforter. Sure, he was Cousin Petey's dad, but it didn't even hurt to admit. He was a legend, the most famous pastor in Oregon, and maybe one of its most famous people. A church tens of thousands strong. A church that had burst through the seams in a place so far from any real population that it was rightly considered a miracle.

The Smiths would trundle down often, as any excuse to escape Coos Bay for a weekend was a good excuse, especially after Nana and Grampy pulled up stakes again and moved to Southern California. Cousin Petey and I would play Conquest of the Empire, walk to the nearby elementary school and swing on the jungle gym, torment our sisters by making them punch trees in the yard, and get in trouble.

Then Sunday morning would roll around. Uncle Jonny would be out early; we'd follow and catch service two or three, never one, since it began at 8:00, and never four, since it ended mid-afternoon and we'd still have to make the curvy four-hour trip back home.

In summer, there were only two services, since there was plenty of room in a gorgeously massive outdoor amphitheater, fresh flowers planted each week around the stage, fresh turf maintained with baseball stadium–esque attention, oaks and willows sprouting among worshipers who would arrive in the middle of the prior service and huddle within striking distance so as to be able to lay blankets and towels down on the most desirable terraced step.

Half the amphitheater would be shaded for the majority of the service, the other half in what Oregon considered blazing sun. The shaded half was prime territory, but Uncle Jonny would recognize the commitment of those on the sunny side and give them more attention, praising their fortitude, good-naturedly laughing at their pain when he went long, which he did every service.

There was a cool bath waiting at the end, at least for the unsaved. The amphitheater also featured a babbling brook that fed a waist-deep pool directly in front of the stage. After preaching, praying, preach-praying while the worship band strummed worship, Uncle Jonny would call on those who had come to meet the Lord during the service and, with Aimee Semple McPherson flair, hop into that pool fully clothed.

Baptism is, of course, serious business across the Christian spectrum, representing our death to sin and being reborn to eternal life—an essential rite never dismissed nor devalued. And while Catholics sprinkle their children, Presbyterians smear with a wet hand, and Baptists fully dunk in public swimming pools on set calendar dates, it is the Charismatics who rule this game. Aimee Semple McPherson would plunge crowds into the waters of the Holy Spirit, and Pastor Chuck Smith, alongside Lonnie Frisbee, would dunk in Orange County's Pirate's Cove. Uncle Jonny would baptize anywhere—any river, any ocean, any lake—but Applegate Christian Fellowship's service-ending spectacle was perfection.

Hot sun blazing overhead, sweat streaming down his furrowed brow, he would raise a strong hand that nodded toward his high school years spent throwing discus, eyes screwed tightly shut, preach-praying to the crowd filling the amphitheater to overflowing. People everywhere, even some in the trees as a wink to the roots.

He would expertly tie the sermon's main thrust into a classic altar call, that Jesus died for our sins and all we have to do is accept his gift, and then hop down from the stage into the waist-deep pool, usually wearing linen pants and a linen button-up shirt, sometimes wearing cargo pants and a short-sleeved button-up. And the people would cascade toward him, ushers and helpers there to sort the chaos into semi-orderly winding lines.

As each sinner waded in fully clothed, Uncle Jonny would talk warmly with them, often clutching the back of their heads with his strong hand and pulling them close, a remarkable display of personal love. He would pray over them, walk them through accepting Jesus Christ as their personal Lord and savior, dunk them, hug them, then help guide them to an usher or helper waiting with a towel and a King James Bible.

Hours.

It would go on for hours, and I would sit on one of the empty grass steps and watch in pure awe. It was magical. Uncle Jonny doing the Lord's work, famously. I joined the line myself, one hot summer's day when I was twelve or thirteen, and he clutched the back of my head, pulling me close. "Charlie, the Lord loves you so much that he sacrificed his only begotten son so that He can be with you forever . . ." Beautiful and true, though I had become a Christian a decade earlier and quietly wondered if Uncle Jonny thought I was a naughty unbeliever all those long years. After I was dunked, I got a new King James Bible too, and added it to my vast collection.

In autumn, winter, and spring, when southern Oregon's weather is reliably terrible, the four Sunday services would take place in the newly built sanctuary, and while there were no spectacular baptisms, every New Year's Eve ushered in the most important day on Applegate Christian Fellowship's calendar.

The sanctuary would begin filling at least two hours prior to that evening service. Men in sport sandals and rolled-sleeve T-shirts tucked into corduroy shorts clutching well-worn brown leather King James Bibles chatting with men in casual sweatshirts, corduroy pants, Birkenstocks clutching well-worn brown leather King James Bibles chatting with women in below-the-knee jean skirts paired with ankle boots and lovingly feathered bangs clutching King James Bibles that had been used just as vigorously as the men's but showed no sign of wear. The women's Bibles, sheathed in embroidered carrying cases, also had the last three weeks' worth of sermon notes inside—marked up, underlined, underlined twice for emphasis, exclamation marks after insights meant to stick.

Even though the conversations were warm and smiles broad, a perceptible tension ran through the air. The sanctuary was always full on autumn, winter, and spring Sundays, stretching beyond its 2,500-person capacity for each of the day's four services and the two evening services. It was often full for Wednesday's Bible study and near full on Monday, Tuesday, Thursday, and Friday for various worship services and guest Bible studies, but December 31 it packed to overflowing early, with no second or third options to fall back on.

New Year's Eve was when Uncle Jonny delivered his much-anticipated yearly prophecy update, and to miss it—to miss insights into current world events and how they related to the return of Christ—was unthinkable.

"Revelation has a unique promise attached to it," he would say any time he came to the final book of the Bible on Sundays or Wednesdays, especially every New Year's Eve, holding his well-worn brown leather King James Bible wide with discus-strong arms.

"Let's look at verse three of chapter one together, for here it says, 'Blessed is he that readeth, and they that hear the words of this prophecy, and keep those things which are written therein: for the time is at hand.'" His words, slow and loud, each one punctuated with exaggerated expressions. Eyes crinkling warmly.

Mouth smiling wide. "This book promises that anyone who reads or even hears it receives a blessing . . ."

The worship band would finish their final guitar tunings in front of the large wood carving of a descending dove. Stylized but instantly recognizable to the Calvary faithful. Along with preaching linearly through the Word, Calvary Chapel's unique spin on evangelicalism was to feature the dove, representing the Holy Spirit descending from heaven, more prominently than the traditional cross. A few bolder men in the sanctuary had the dove tattooed on an ankle, right above a sport sandal strap or Birkenstock strap.

A lucky few remained standing, chatting, drinking coffee from tall thermos cups until the last minute always. They didn't have to panic sit, as they had husbands, wives, mothers, or fathers saving a space on the pew with King James Bibles, either well-worn brown leather or sheathed.

All the Bibles, every single one, were the King James Version. That is what Uncle Jonny used exclusively, and that's what the church's bookstore sold exclusively, with a few New King James Versions for the kids next to Psalty the Singing Songbook cassette tapes and Jon Courson Bible Commentaries compiled, edited, and made to glow, literarily, by my mother.

The stilted language—thees, thous, thines—directly opposed the purposefully casual air of Applegate Christian Fellowship's amphitheater and its sanctuary, with its earth-toned interiors, large windows highlighting southern Oregon's pastoral charm, descending dove instead of cross, and lack of pulpit on the stage where the worship band spread into position. Worship leader behind microphone, acoustic guitar with modified amplifier plugged into amp on his right side. Bass player hiking his bass high and tight slightly behind him, slightly awkwardly. Number one background vocalist, female, holding her tambourine at the ready. Number two female vocalist, holding her tambourine by her side. Drummer seated at the kit, sticks resting on the snare drum, and bongo player next to him on a higher stool, hands on hips.

The praise music would fill the air without warning. A classic Maranatha! song, "He Is Exalted," reverberating over pews and into hearts. Or maybe the classic Maranatha! song "Glorify Thy Name." Everyone in the sanctuary instantly on their feet, some with one hand raised, open palm to heaven. Some with both hands. More eyes closed than not. Maranatha! Music was Calvary Chapel's worship music arm, churning out hit after hit after hit, shaming generations of musicians—Three Dog Night, Three Doors Down, plus every other band that thought it was building a catalog.

My eyes wide open, breath caught in mouth, those lucky New Year's Eves the Smiths crashed Applegate Christian Fellowship's greatest show on earth, along with all the cousins, Nana, Grampy, Uncle Dave, etc. and standing in the most enviable position of all.

Having a spot in a pew mattered, as opposed to being relegated to the cursed overflow room with its first-generation big-screen television, and where that pew was also mattered. Being too far back, or worse, back corner, signaled a lack of seriousness, of consideration. Middle-back was fine, but middle-middle was better, practically perfect, and middle-front was as desirable as it was fraught with danger, for middle-front was for people who truly belonged. The husbands and wives of the worship team. Various youth pastors and Bible study heavies; if a visitor accidentally thought, "I should sit middle-front and get the best experience possible," they would have many eye daggers shot their way until the only available option would be to shuffle away, pretending to need the restroom or some such.

When the entire Courson clan was in attendance, there was no room for even husbands and wives of the worship team or various youth pastors and Bible study heavies. Nana wouldn't even shoot eye daggers, but would march straight up and clear the front two pews with a stern but warm, "All my kids are here." Interlopers would bow their heads and muddle quickly away as if Cousin Queen Elizabeth herself had shamed them, and we'd slide into our respective slots, usually in birth order beginning with Cousin Danny, ending with Cousin Benny, who was still in diapers.

People would come pay fealty, and I'd dip my head, as if I deserved it, soaking in the fame until the classic Maranatha! song "He Has Made Me Glad" filled the air and everyone scrambled to their King James Bible–saved spaces.

Before the worship band finished, Uncle Jonny would take the stage, singing loud and off-key, slower than the actual beat, eyes closed, holding his well-worn brown leather King James Bible wide with strong arms, transitioning the song into a prayer, riffing on the promises of Revelation and then digging in, tying global events directly into Biblical prophecy from the books of Revelation, of course, but also Daniel, Hosea, Amos, and Obadiah, with bobs and weaves into Habakkuk and even Nahum.

Everything made sense: the rise and fall of the Soviet Union; collapse of the Berlin Wall; the coalescing of a European Union and march toward one world currency; King Juan Carlos of Spain's ascension to the throne. Everything tied into an already written narrative. I'd hang on every word, only taking brief pauses to doodle surfing men on the offertory envelopes and looking up and down the row to see all the cousins paying serious attention.

We cousins would joke among ourselves, regularly, about who was Nana's favorite, placing ourselves on a sort of Ladder of Divine Ascent, simply calling it "Nana's Ladder." Cousin Danny, being the first-born grandchild, good at math, on the way to being a Navy Top Gun or astronaut, handsome and slightly awkward, a practiced smile, eager eyes, was always on top. He had a polished way with adults that wowed me at a very early age. Able to spin stories of whatever he was working on at school, whatever he was playing in sports, into engaging but appropriately humble fodder. He seemed to become near-perfect in the presence of uncles, aunts, grandparents, and other churchgoing adults.

He was nose guard on the high school football team, and I assumed, from hearing Nana describe it, that nose guard was the most important position of all. Better than any quarterback, running back, wide receiver, linebacker, safety—even though I was a football fan and knew it wasn't. Such was the Courson descriptive power, though, elevating a middling defensive line position to the lofty heights of true power. He later played water polo, and while I don't remember his position, I'm certain it was equally important.

When we kids were alone, with uncle, aunt, or parent off discussing Republican politics or which of their high school teachers was weirdest, Cousin Mikey would goad his brother, Cousin Danny, into a fine rage. They fought differently than my sister, brother, and me. Our battles were small, usually about Emily walking down the stairs in her bathrobe faux-accidentally knocking Andy and my G.I. Joe setups down. Oh how it infuriated us, but before we could really get at it, our mother would swoop in quickly with her "it takes two to fight but one to make peace" lecture. Getting along with each other was the most important of the rules.

Cousins Danny and Mikey fought like the cool teenagers on *Saved by the Bell*. Really digging in, with harsh personal and physical jabs. Proper mean. Cousin Mikey, particularly, who had a real way of saying and doing just the right things to get an over-blown, uncontrolled reaction. I'd watch, saucer-eyed, waiting for the harshest recriminations from their parents, but they never came. No stern talking-tos, just a "knock it off, you two" light hand.

They'd really get into it when no adults had any hope of hearing. There was an eclectic landowner near Cousins Danny and Mikey's faux-Tudor with a large plot near one of Carlsbad's lagoons. The property was mostly open, and we were free to wander, but the best part was that it had a duplex cage. A monkey lived in one half. A lion lived in the other. We would regularly head down, alone, to pet the monkey and the lion, and Cousin Mikey would go all in on Cousin Danny, winding him up until he would stomp away alone.

A monkey and a lion sharing a duplex cage with ocean views that children could pet made perfect sense back then, and was as inspiring as boogie boarding, surfing, warm water jetties, being cool, fighting dirty.

Inevitably, when we left their house and made our way back to depressing Oregon, I would get in big trouble for "acting like Mikey" in how I treated my sister. The long lecture would build into an intense crescendo.

Cousin Mikey and I were closer in age. He boogie-boarded better than Cousin Danny and had a cooler surf style, always in just the right Gotcha sweatshirt or Flojos sandals. When the uncles, aunts, or parents were present, he would maintain a sort of sarcastic, vaguely mocking vibe that awed me. Cousin Danny never did any of that. He was pure polished humility, eagerly asking the right questions with the right tone of voice. Something seemed fake about it to me, since I saw the way he and Cousin Mikey fought. Cousin Danny seemed to be playing a game—a smarter game that positively worked. Danny was destined for greatness, carrying the Courson torch in the exact way it was supposed to be carried.

Nana's favorite.

Continuing down her ladder came my sister Emily, or Emmy to all the cousins, second-born but the first granddaughter, also smart, also tall, driven, dynamic, and forever nipping at Cousin Danny's heels. Uncle Jonny's kids swapped positions near the top, especially Cousin Petey, who seemed bound for the ministry, and also played nose guard on his high school football team. Uncle Jimmy's three were always up there too, as they were missionary kids helping serve the Lord at a Mexican orphanage.

I was near the bottom. Always. There was no specific way to know that I was down there, but the feeling hung heavy. Nana, for instance, had instituted an epic reward early on in all our lives that each cousin would get one week with her and Grampy, spoiled with late-night Chex Mix and shopping sprees. Cousins Danny and Mikey got their weeks, my sister got hers, Cousin Petey got his, and then it was my turn, except the program was mysteriously canceled without explanation, only to be picked up again with Cousin Petey's younger sister, Cousin Jessie.

Even though I was not Nana's favorite, nor was my brother, Andy, whose Christian rock band drummer attire, featuring super-baggy tiger-print pants and a headband, confounded her, this second generation of cousins was making good on its promise of Christian greatness. "Rebellion" consisted of Cousin Mikey talking back to his parents, slamming his bedroom door once, and buying a parrot. My sister Emily wanting to date a guy who went to our Marshfield High School and was much older than a typical high school student, plus drove a red motor scooter. Cousin Petey might have purchased a "secular" Bryan Adams cassette, and I had amassed a good stack of Garbage Pail Kids that got discovered and pitched, followed by an extremely serious lecture.

Only one earthquake shook the foundation of my young world—and it wasn't even when Uncle Jonny heavily suggested that King Juan Carlos of Spain *could* be the Antichrist. In retrospect, clearly a hot read, but that's what made his prophecy updates such a hit. The bridging between the ancient and today via truth and mystery. We all carry a skeptical arrogance, like we know cold, hard, observable truths. Science, the academy, etc., has debunked childish mysteries, but we know next to nothing, let's be honest. We know nothing at all, and if the Lord tarries, even that nothing will seem as foolish as tying rats to our necks in order to stave off the Black Plague in three hundred years. King Juan Carlos abdicated the throne in 2014 without exhibiting any overtly satanic tendencies, and is still alive as of this writing, not pushing a one-world currency. The event that rocked me, rather, was an idyllic Courson family reunion on the Valley Isle of Maui.

I was thirteen and couldn't believe this fortunate turn in my life. My parents, while wonderful, generous, and kind, were not wealthy. Vacations consisted of driving California's coast each summer, camping along the way, ending up with Cousins Danny and Mikey for a few days, watching missionary slideshows, eating Jiffy Pop, then flipping and heading home. Going on an airplane to Maui, staying at the Embassy Suites, getting a rental car, was a luxury only ever dared dreamed.

The initial offering seemed otherworldly. Beyond belief. My mother designed and printed matching pink T-shirts for everyone—all the uncles, aunts, cousins—that declared "Courson Family Reunion" in a squiggly *Malcolm in the Middle* font, and I counted the days until we jumped in the van, whispering a prayer that it wouldn't break down along the way, for the fifteen-hour drive south to Los Angeles International Airport, where everyone was meeting.

We zipped past Medford, Shasta, Willows, Stockton, over the Grapevine, craning our necks at Magic Mountain and dreaming of what those roller coasters must feel like, then pulled into our airport-adjacent hotel; our flight to Maui was departing early the next morning.

Uncle Jonny and his family, Uncle Jimmy and his, were already there, having flown like normal people, and we tittered with the cousins, wondering when Uncle Dave and his family would arrive.

They did, apparently, late at night, when we were in bed watching rare cable television, and there was some odd commotion requiring help from the uncles. The next morning, as we shuttled to the airport, I noticed Aunt Kris wasn't there and that Cousins Danny and Mikey seemed taciturn. They were both deep into high school, and I wondered if it was just teen surliness, though that didn't explain Aunt Kris's absence.

Before we got on the plane, we were told quietly that Uncle Dave and Aunt Kris were having a few problems, but not to worry because the Courson Family Reunion was kicking off and we'd soon all be at the Embassy Suites.

Oh the Kaanapali Embassy Suites with its pink-hued mid-1970s Brutalist towers tickling the blue sky, palm trees swaying in the warm trade winds, parrot in an open-air lobby that posed for pictures, swimming pool featuring a real waterslide, free peanuts (both regular and honey-roasted) served in that open-air lobby every happy hour—but we Coursons didn't drink alcohol, nor did we Smiths, so we changed the name to "peanut hour."

I had never seen anything so glorious in my entire life, and to be there as part of this famous clan made it that much better. We would all meet at "peanut hour" every midafternoon, in paradise, each family around their own table happily munching honey-roasted peanuts, and receive the run of show for the next day. "Tomorrow, precious children and grandchildren, we are going to ride the sugarcane train . . ." Nana would say while clasping her hands together, charm bracelet jingling. Or "Tomorrow, precious children and grandchildren, we have hired a world-renowned photographer and will be taking a family picture on the rocks at sunset."

Everything was superlative with Nana because it was. The best, fanciest, most. And all the Coursons oooh'd and ahhh'd at the extravagance, except Cousins Danny and Mikey had continued the general off-ness first exhibited in Los Angeles. They were trying to be polite, kind—especially to Nana and Grampy—but rumors floated among the rest of the cousins that they had somehow been forced to come. That Uncles Jonny and Jimmy had been called in to help secure Cousin Danny before he could bolt from the airport hotel. That there had been some other physical altercation in the Embassy Suites.

The parents, uncles, and aunts kept their lips zipped, as was the Courson way. Topics of conversation around the tables during "peanut hour" included Republican politics, my brother Andy's probable Christian rock 'n' roll future, Nana getting faux angry at my father for saying lightly inappropriate things (as cheer kings do), the possibility of European countries joining in some union and its relevance to the book of Revelations, the following day's plan and highlights from Willie "The Say-Hey Kid" Mays's mid-1960s San Francisco Giants days. The only mentions of Aunt Kris's absence were quietly brushed over and only quickly whispered "problems" associated with "ladies in the church who had gotten her ear and were causing them." That was it.

One day, we woke up early, climbed into our rented, matching gray Toyota Corolla station wagons, drove to a nearby trailhead, and hiked into what felt like a jungle wonderland. Sandalwood, koa, and banyan trees with roots bursting through the red earth as if they were tracks of roller coasters. If *Jurassic Park* had been released, I would have thought the Coursons stumbled right onto the set.

The cousins fanned out, mouths agape, exploring, trying to keep the red earth off my pink and teal Tevas, until we all stumbled upon a pile of candy in the crook of two banyan roots. Full-size Charleston Chews, king-size Snickers, Skittles, unfortunate Almond Joys and Mounds (Nana's favorite), Now and Laters, Laffy Taffy, Goo Goo Clusters, boring M&Ms, peanut M&Ms, and Almond Roca in their gold foil.

Uncle Jimmy gasped, exaggeratedly, and pointed at the treasure trove, the youngest cousins jumping into the spoils while the rest of the uncles and aunts stood around smiling. Like everything, though, there was an object lesson attached to this luxurious find, and we were all told to sit around in a semicircle while Uncle Dave took his place in our middle.

"You know," he hyper-enunciated, "you are all mighty children of God on a grand adventure . . ."

Off he went through the stories of Joshua, David, the Apostle Paul, John of Patmos, tying it all back into the candy windfall at our feet. It was a moving sermon and appreciated by all, except Cousins Danny and Mikey, who stood off to the side looking downright furious. I assumed their rage was directly related to both the Almond Joys and Mounds, two of the worst candies ever made, but couldn't be sure.

Something, though, was now definitely wrong. Fundamentally bent in a way that the Coursons didn't ever bend. I kept my legs crisscrossed, listening to Uncle Dave, raptish, but kept Cousins Danny and Mikey in my periphery. Especially Cousin Danny, as his face was twisted into an almost cinematic sneer.

CHAPTER 6

OF CINDER BLOCK MAUSOLEUMS AND MEN

Growing up a pastor's kid, or a missionary kid, is an entire class known well to evangelical Christians since the church, and the mission field is central to life. The pastor's kid is generally on top of a vast social hierarchy as a young child. Adored and doted on by the congregation. Number one, and most popular, in Sunday School; quick on the draw during drills, exercises where the Bible is held aloft, the Sunday School teacher names a verse, the Bibles are dropped down, vigorously opened, and the first student to find it wins; first picked in Awana summer camp games, like "Crazy Relays" or "Keep Your Yard Clean," where balls of crumbled paper were tossed from a circle.

Awana (Approved Workmen Are Not Ashamed) is a children's church program that's an extension of Sunday School. In my mind it was like Christian Boy Scouts/Girl Scouts, utilizing strictly Native American categorizations like "brave" and "chief" to show advancement instead of the Boy Scouts's random mash of "tenderfoot" and "eagle palm."

Pastors' kids are also routinely and prominently cast in Psalty the Singing Songbook or *Hi-Tops* musical productions. *Hi-Tops*, distributed by Calvary Chapel's Maranatha! Music imprint, told the story of three angels sent to earth to study peer pressure and fight Satan for hearts and minds.

If the pastor's church is large, the pastor's kid will have more cachet but also more pressure and more duties. They will have to be on perpetual best behavior. As a representative of leadership, there will be no room for fidgeting during services. They will also have to attend multiple services regularly, and stay until the last person has sipped the last of their coffee from a Styrofoam cup, eaten their last donut hole. They will have to stand next to pastor/father (it was always a father), smile smeared across face, until the very last hand had been shaken.

My best friend in the world, Josh, was a PK, or pastor's kid, and described himself as "King Nerd of Awana. Spark, Brave, Chief. Three books all in one year, then I punched the Awana bully in the face and gave him a bloody lip and we were, after that, unstoppable rulers. Then moved."

His pastor/father was an itinerant.

The missionary kid has cachet on the field, as foreign lands are called, but is often reentered into the western world in awkward ways and at awkward times. Coming back on "furlough," for instance, to travel and speak in various churches in order to share wonderful news of successes and converts, churches built, languages translated into Bibles.

My other best friend in the world, Nate, was a MK and told me, "I won the Timothy Award for Oansa." Oansa? Confused, I asked him if Oansa was the off-brand foreign version of Awana, and he replied, "Yes, a missionary couple made it their deal. *Obreros Aprobados No Son Avergonzados.*" In English: "Approved Workers Are Not Ashamed."

Both pastor's kids and missionary kids are expected, by the world at large, to "backslide" at some point in postpubescent life, i.e., dancing or drinking, smoking or partaking in other frowned-upon behavior, including, but not limited to, cursing properly. Shucking off all that pressure and expectation for a worldly jig. And it is further assumed both will lose religion entirely later in life, as religion is clearly an opiate for the masses and dumb.

Cousin Danny occupied an odd space in between. His father was a missionary, officially, but Cousin Danny lived his day-to-day in Carlsbad, California, in a faux-Tudor and not on some exotic Mosquito Coast. Not gazing up at a slash in the Himalayas leading into Afghanistan, donkeys braying, Stinger missiles waiting, palling around with proto-Taliban, basically Islam's version of Awana minus Native American categorizations.

Still, he would go on the ubiquitous church-speaking tours with his father, sit in the front row, and pretend to listen attentively as Uncle Dave shared the great news of his Christian Emergency Relief Team work. Knowing that the eyes of the congregation were on him. Cousin Danny would nod earnestly, even though he'd heard the three sermons his father rotates through regularly, and especially the "Mighty Men of God" one.

It was motivational—all of Uncle Dave's sermons were—but this was the most motivational of all, focusing on the underdogs, the unexpected, the small, unfit, odd people that God chooses to work through. The young shepherd David, who killed a giant and became king. The fugitive Moses, on the run from Egyptian law for killing a guard. Jonah, who ran directly from God's command to preach to the undesirables; the apostle Peter, who denied Christ three times; the apostle Paul who put early Christians to death, etc.

After moving through the Old Testament then the New, Uncle Dave would tell the story of his best friend from Vietnam. About how he and Tom had come under fire in what would later be referred to as "the greatest artillery barrage in the Vietnam War."

The small hum of Bibles being flipped through, purses being searched for gum, would stop entirely, and Uncle Dave would lower his voice, slowly describing the most heroic night ever when Tom, a modern-day Mighty Man of God, hurled himself onto a live grenade for the platoon.

Eyes would fill with tears as Uncle Dave encouraged each person to become a Mighty Man of God. To join CERT on an upcoming mission or, if that wasn't possible, to support the cause financially.

Cousin Danny claims now that he watched this show cynically. Watched his father soak up what he calls "his drug of attention getting slammed into a vein, coursing through larger and larger tubes until it hit his heart, then jet-boosted to his brain, flooding it with dopamine, serotonin, epinephrine. You can almost see his head tilt back just a hair, like a new heroin user feeling the hit." That his father didn't really believe what he was saying and he, Cousin Danny, was really only looking forward to going to McDonald's afterward and was put off by the artificiality of his father's pitch. Even more, that he recognized his own bank-robbing fugitive future in Uncle Dave's prying money from church folk to pay for wild adventures. But hindsight is an easily manipulated animal and that, to me, is a stretch.

Uncle Dave believes and always has and always will.

Soon after the Courson family reunion on Maui, Cousin Danny graduated high school, the first of the cousins to do so. And even though he says now that he was disgusted by his father's life, having just watched him go through an ugly divorce from his mother, my Aunt Kris, that he was, in fact, a missionary kid who had lost his religion, he didn't run, cynically, to Oberlin College, or any other iconic coeducational institution of higher learning specializing in nonbinary sexual exploration for the religiously jaded. The whole Aunt Kris business went unresolved, more or less, other than the narrative of those crafty "ladies in the church who had gotten her ear" and pushed her directly into that great Christian evil of "divorce," but that didn't stop Cousin Danny from enrolling at the Nazarene institute of higher learning, Point Loma University in nearby La Jolla.

At first, I was very dubious about the Nazarenes' true faithfulness to the Word of God. I knew that Jesus had been raised in the town of Nazareth, even once visiting the fine Palestinian town myself, but the word sounded weird, a little suspicious, and I wondered if the Nazarenes did weird stuff like the Seventh-day Adventists, having church on Saturday or whatnot.

In truth, they grew out of the same Holiness movement that captivated Nana, grew Aimee Semple McPherson, formed the foundation of Uncle Dave, Uncle Jonny, and my mother's Biola, and led directly to the foundation of Pastor Chuck Smith's Calvary Chapel.

I went to Biola too, following that proud Courson tradition that now included my older sister, who left her very-much-older boyfriend still magically in high school and moved into the all-girls dorm Alpha Chi the year before I snuck into the all-boys dorm Emerson Hall under "probation," seeing as my Marshfield High School grades were very poor.

Like Uncle Jonny before me, I spent a significant amount of time at Calvary Chapel Costa Mesa, except all at the behest of my Biola roommate. He had a car, loved *The Andy Griffith Show*, and revered the Calvary pastors as saints, cataloging and relistening to his favorites of their sermons, constantly putting us to sleep with Calvary Chapel's radio station, K-Wave, turned too loud.

By then it was considered a "megachurch," and I wanted to love it too, wanted to feel the adjacent Courson fame, but the general aesthetic of its late-1980s sanctuary were visually painful. Oversized pizza parlor–esque lights hanging from a too-low ceiling. Lavish use of glass bricks. Etc.

Biola had thrice-weekly chapels, a requisite Bible minor, a "behavior contract" featuring a pledge not to drink, smoke, or dance—all mandatory for students to sign every single year. In comparison, Point Loma was seen as "liberal" because its students didn't have to minor in Bible and had more gracious visiting hours in the dorms—still couldn't smoke, drink, or dance, though. At Biola, boys could see girls in their dorms one day a week for three hours, and vice versa. Point Loma had an enviable *nightly* three-hour window, and during a few of those chaste-but-bubbling-with-hormones hours, Cousin Danny's fiancée, Mandi, would visit. They had met at church and fallen in love as seventeen-year-olds, signed evangelical abstinence advocate Josh McDowell's "True Love Waits" pledge, married at twenty as sophomores, and danced to Art Garfunkel's cover of "I Only Have Eyes for You" at their wedding before heading off to an exciting honeymoon (reprising Maui), then returning to Point Loma, where Cousin Danny worked as a resident assistant in one of the dorms, guiding his juniors into the fruitful life.

Except the marriage didn't flow quite so easily. His young wife, he felt, wasn't emotional enough. Didn't reach for him enough. Simply wanted a robotic man of God who looked good on paper but had no fire inside. Cousin Danny, on the other hand, knew what he wanted. Craved passion, desire, headless rushes into wild embraces at the end of the day.

Passion.

He also knew he didn't really know what he was talking about, and began chalking up the small failures, the overall frigidity, to the abstinence pledges, contracts with Christian colleges and universities, and pressure from the church to "stay pure" by hosting staged musical performances on Wednesday nights that highlighted the dangers of sex outside of marriage.

They were all tacky and silly, granted—a horrible modern evangelical reimagining of ancient morality, except even when hideously bastardized, that ancient morality actually makes some sense, or at least more sense than our modern, selfish godlessness.

However turgid Cousin Danny and his young wife felt in their blessed relationship, however frustrated, a gloriously, perpetually rosy picture was painted to the rest of the family. Danny was the first of the youngest generation to marry, and he worked hard at Point Loma, earning top marks with the goal of attending medical school after graduation and becoming a doctor. Not quite an astronaut but very honorable.

I was keeping busy with my own Intercultural Studies at Biola, the missionary-in-training degree. Bible minor, chapels, Torrey Memorial Bible Conference week, Mission week, and once-a-semester whimsical GYRADs—"Get Your Roommate a Date" nights usually featuring Pizookie pizza cookies from BJ's Restaurant or maybe bowling/laser tag.

Alas, Cousin Danny didn't do quite well enough on his MCATs and was forced to pivot to a nursing degree, though he was accepted into a respected program all the way across the country, at Rutgers in New Jersey in the mid-2000s. A Scarlet Knight dragging his young family to New Brunswick.

The whole business caught me flatfooted, I'll be very honest. "Cousin Danny is becoming a nurse?" I asked my sister, who delivered me the news in the middle of Biola's campus next to the outdoor student mailbox with a visual aesthetic oddly similar to Mecca's Kaaba. A large square with students circumambulating during specified between-class hours.

She nodded with a smirk on her face. She was just beginning to see cracks in the glowing Courson narrative, and seemed to be reveling in it. She was editor in chief of Biola's newspaper, as a sophomore, and was defining her journalistic chops by gumshoeing real stories and fighting the powers that be in administration.

"Nurse Danny?"

She stifled another laugh.

But these were the first cracks I'd ever seen in the glowing Courson narrative, besides Uncle Dave's divorce from Aunt Kris. The ugly Maui business had been entirely quashed, and his new wife, Aunt Terry, appeared out of nowhere. She seemed nice enough, though nobody spent too much time with her, as Uncle Dave swept her off to live in Vanuatu almost immediately after their wedding. Vanuatu seemed entirely exotic, some place Uncle Dave should certainly go in order to save people, and Aunt Kris's "ladies in the church" had really blown it for her, stealing an exotic

South Pacific island lifestyle, replete with building churches, pulling teeth, and preaching the Word.

Nurse-in-training Cousin Danny seemed a clear fall, though. A "shoot for the moon even if you miss it and you'll land among the stars" mockery, because no nurses had ever been stars outside of Florence Nightingale, Dorothea Dix, Clara Barton, and . . . now that I think of it, a whole host of others. But no male nurses, save Saint Camillus de Lila, Edward Lyon, and Joe Hogan . . . but I digress! Astronaut to doctor to nurse was rough in the light of the surrounding famous pastors and famous missionaries.

Though it was there, in New Brunswick, New Jersey, shooting for the moon and hitting the dirt, that Cousin Danny's future as a record-nearing, if not record-setting, bank robber had another important growth spurt: evangelical Republican birth and upbringing, with all that inventive non-naughtiness, combined with the glorious freedom of Protestantism.

"Works" were for Catholics. Thinking that it was somehow possible to "earn" God's absolution through our own small offerings. Going to confession, getting assigned Hail Marys, feeling bad. *Faith* was for us. Faith and grace. The Apostle Paul wrote, in his second letter to the early Christians living in Corinth (King James Version), "All things are lawful unto me, but all things are not expedient: all things are lawful for me, but I will not be brought under the power of any."

All things are lawful to me, to us, and sure, smoking, drinking, dancing, etc. are fenced off with "purity pledges" because they are certainly not expedient, but whatever. No Hail Marys. Little to no guilt.

Except Cousin Danny discovered alcohol and dancing while at Rutgers. Republican rule-toying combined with evangelical grace combined with booze and hip shaking. It would have all been fine and good, maybe, except Cousin Danny's wife did not buy in, as it were. However excessive, prudish, out-of-touch, weird—*Christian*—her frustration over "goofy fun and innocent" dance-floor grinding (as he later described it to me) and drinking seemed, those two alone have felled many a "secular" marriage. Those and money, or the lack thereof.

In college debt and away from family, Cousin Danny finished his nursing degree without getting into more apparent trouble and whisked his wife back to North County, San Diego, getting work in a few local hospitals, buying a nice suburban home in Vista, just inland of Carlsbad and once the seat of much Cousin Danny and Cousin Mikey scorn.

As boogie-boarding kids, they did not care for Vista, Escondido, San Marcos, or any other non-coastline-touching municipalities where "barneys"—or surf-illiterate try-hards—lived. Nor did they care for Zonies (from Arizona) and would spit the word with pure disdain when we'd drive to Warm Water Jetty in those idyllic early years. "So many *Zonies* on the beach today . . ." while scanning the packed sand and parking lot filled with dusty red Grand Canyon State license plates. Me, eyes darting, thankful that I was not from Arizona, but Oregon, which somehow escaped their wrath.

Beggars can't be choosers, though, and soon after the Vista repatriation came Cousin Danny and his wife's baby boy, the first Courson great-grandchild. He brought much joy to Nana, and assurance that the famous Courson line would extend into a whole new generation. Baby Caleb could be anything. A famous pastor. A famous missionary. A famous pastor. Obviously, a Republican. Hopefully not a nurse, but even a nurse could become a doctor in Nana's glorious curly cursive missives.

She'd write semiregularly to my Biola Kaaba mailbox. Glowing reports of Cousin Danny, his graduating top of his class, being accepted to one of San Diego's premier hospitals and having a son, cracks in the Courson narrative deftly spackled. Of Cousin Mikey becoming the best Porsche mechanic in the entire western United States. Of Cousin Petey excelling at Calvary Chapel's Bible college in Murrieta, set to follow in his father's glorious footprints and of the rest of the cousins too, their various wins and wins.

A century of Courson greatness pushed boldly into the next century without buckle or hitch. Not even from new Aunt Terry, who had fled her exotic South Pacific island paradise on the pretense of caring for her ailing father back home in the States, but then refused to go back and demanded her union with Uncle Dave be ended with the swiftest of divorces.

That bit of news trickled out slowly, with light head-shaking and not much discussion beyond it clearly being Aunt Terry's fault. My sister, Emily, who was studying to become an actual newspaper journalist, an almost extinct sort with dedication to tirelessly getting the story and getting it right, was not satisfied with this at all and elicited the fact that Uncle Jimmy had had to fly to Vanuatu a few months after Aunt Terry left, on directive from Uncle Jonny, to "fetch" Uncle Dave. When he arrived, he allegedly found a cinder block mausoleum that Uncle Dave had constructed filled with reams and reams of top-secret CIA papers. Uncle Jimmy had had to drag Uncle Dave away, and even those dribs and drabs were crazy hard to come by. I had never loved Uncle Dave more.

He had been my north star, my Indiana Jones. Suddenly he was also my Allie Fox, beautifully played by the same Harrison Ford, in *The Mosquito Coast*. A perfect man, possessed with adventure, Aunt Kris and his new Aunt Terry be damned, especially since Aunt Kris once got mad at me for putting the wrong cups in the sink and new Aunt Terry always seemed to be staring off into space and not really aware of the epic, legendary life she was living with.

Cousin Danny may not have appreciated his father's cinematic derring-do as much as I did, but he did make him proud by erasing his overwhelming college debt by entering the Coast Guard Reserve as an officer. Danny was following a proud patriotic Courson tradition, after Grampy fighting Imperial Japan in the Pacific as a naval man and Uncle Dave opting for the jungles of Vietnam as a Marine gunnery sergeant.

But the Coast Guard?

The Coast Guard.

But who was I to criticize? I was spending my days parsing Anton LaVey's *Satanic Bible* in an Introduction to Linguistics class that was supposed to lead to a career in Bible translation. Why in hell was I doing that? To glean insight into secularism's far outposts? To shock a kind Bible translator professor? It was a book so devoid of art or meaning as to be . . . really, really bad. Worth a read for the following passage alone:

> The person who takes every opportunity to "pick on" others is often mistakenly called "sadistic." In reality, this person is a misdirected masochist who is working towards his own destruction.

Very cool, Anton, and I still have no idea why I was treating the *Satanic Bible* as literarily or spiritually important, but there, anyhow, by the grace of God, went Cousin Danny.

CHAPTER 7

MOHEGAN SUN

Cousin Danny had been looking forward to the three weeks' training session on the other side of the country at the Coast Guard Academy in Connecticut for a good while—not that he necessarily enjoyed his Coast Guard service, the impending training, the saluting and being saluted. His dad, Uncle Dave, was proud of him, and that made it even more ridiculous, as all he saw was artifice. Cheap epaulets and antiquated titles. But three weeks away, on the other side of the country, felt like sweet relief.

His wife had continued to pull away from him physically, to agitate at his going out after work for a few beers, and then, when checking his computer one day, she found the URL of a pornography website in the browser history.

Cousin Danny came home that day to a cold fury he had not yet seen. A freezing ball of rage. He tried to apologize, promised to begin attending marriage counseling sessions at church, swore he had stumbled but would become the man of God, was the man of God, she had chosen.

None of it worked to her satisfaction, even though he tried, really tried, by going to coffee with other men at the church so he could be "held accountable," attending men's group Bible studies regularly, attending those marriage counseling sessions at church. But in his telling, her face remained a chilled mask, her body a chunk of ice, and he was feeling both broken but hardened. That his wife was unreasonable. He loved her still, and loved their son, but given the circumstances at home, those three weeks away were welcome.

Cousin Danny needed a break.

The first two weeks in Connecticut were a dull bore, though he did feel free to drink two beers and browse soft-core porn without recrimination. When his Coastie colleagues told him they were heading out to Mohegan Sun, a gleaming casino that opened in 1996, featuring a tower holding 1,500 rooms and gaming space totaling more than 360,000 square feet, for a night of fabulous gambling, he decided at once to join them.

Slot machines sang their robotic pixie song as soon as he pushed open the glass doors into the "summer entrance." Colored spinning luck wheels, craps tables, poker tables, blackjack tables spread out before him on a patterned blue carpet underneath a giant fiber optic planetarium-like dome. Digital stars twinkled and shone in unison with a crystal tower rising from the floor very near the roulette tables where he, having split from his Coasties, meandered by himself.

Cousin Danny stood and watched the ball spin fast, then slow, before resting in a numbered slot colored black, red, or, rarely, green. He felt his heart beat hard as he imagined where it would land and felt the rush of cheers, the deflation of moans, if he imagined right or wrong. After watching for fifteen or twenty minutes, ordering a beer and nursing it, he marched to the nearest ATM, inserted his card, punched the button next to "savings," then withdrew $500. Exactly half of his and Mandi's nut.

A rush of fire flooded his body.

He had gambled only casually before—low-stakes poker nights at a classmate's house at Rutgers and one time in the Trump Plaza in Atlantic City. Nothing like $500, but he marched to the back of the roulette table like he knew what he was doing, tossed his five crisp $100 bills on the green felt, and asked for one chip.

The dealer was overly compliant, sliding him a purple chip stamped $500, and Cousin Danny studied the numbered grid, getting lost in the options before deciding black was the easiest option. He pushed his chip there and stood back as the wheel started spinning, the rush of fire turning into a jet engine. The ball slowed, bounced, landed on a black number, and his $500 became, like that, $1,000.

Over the next forty-five minutes, he bet the $1,000 limit each turn, all on black. By the time he backed away, he had increased the family savings nearly twenty-fold. A crowd had gathered behind him too, cheering each win, tittering, whispering, oohing and aahing the entire time.

It was absolutely intoxicating, and he felt absolutely intoxicated on the drive back to the Coast Guard Academy with a check for $17,000 in his hand. Coasties drunk and laughing. Cheering. $17,000 instead of $18,000, because he had tossed a $1,000 chip to an admirer at the end of his run, proclaiming her his good-luck charm.

The three-hour time difference even allowed him to call home to share the good news of his incredible run, the great windfall he had brought home from the Mohegan Sun, with his wife. The story was met with icy silence, then a question.

"You bet how much? How could you do that? What if you had lost it all?"

But he hadn't lost it all. He had not only won it all, but won enough to pay off his remaining nursing school debt.

She hung up before he could muster a spirited defense.

Nothing.

Called the next afternoon.

Nothing.

Nothing for the remainder of the week, and he knew he was in trouble again. The flight home seemed eternal. The wait for his baggage everlasting. And when he pushed into San Diego's warm early evening air, there was no wife waiting for him.

He called again.

Nothing.

Nothing.

And so he got a cab and gave directions to his Carlsbad address, glumly cradling his $17,000 check. He and Mandi were in the middle of building a home in Oceanside, thankfully abandoning their Vista dwelling for a proper coastal address. While it was being built, they had rented an apartment a block away from the beach in Carlsbad. He had spent his nonworking hours that summer teaching his five-year-old son to boogie board in the very same waters he had learned upon.

Those were dreamy hours. This was not, and he dreaded the return, knowing that after the weeklong silence and lack of airport ride he was in big, big trouble.

He had no idea how big.

Cousin Danny's cab pulled up to Mandi stuffing the last of her belongings into their Nissan Pathfinder. Their son, strapped into his car seat, brightened upon seeing his dad and chirped, "Daddy! You're back!"

Mandi was less enthusiastic, keeping a frozen face and simply saying, "We're going to my parents' house." And with that, she got in, sparked the ignition, and drove into the night, leaving once and for all.

Cousin Danny stood alone in the driveway long after his family had vanished, hurt, angry, devastated, frustrated. He was working for them, winning for them, and why couldn't his wife see that? What would possess her to leave with their short-term financial problems solved through his bold ingenuity? And his anger grew. His conviction became that *she* was unreasonable, wrong, bent on him being the bad guy no matter what.

Years later, when he told me that winning $17,000 was the last straw in his marriage, it seemed, honestly, positively ludicrous. The Coursons certainly had no gambling tradition; cards were never present at any family gathering, and I have zero idea how to play poker to this day, but it was never preached directly as a no-no, or at least not that I remember.

Gambling was not like booze, like illicit coupling, definitely not derelict like porn, even the soft-core varietal, and in the aftermath of the disentangling of Cousin Danny's marriage to Mandi, his porn thing was whispered about, as were his very naughty trips to strip clubs.

"Well, Cousin Danny . . . went to . . ."—and the already hushed voice quieted even more—". . . to . . ."—basically inaudible—". . . strip clubs."

Proper aghastness ensued, though never proper discussion. But gambling?

Hell, *gambling*?

Again, not one of the deadly sins that I ever heard railed against, but maybe I just wasn't listening or entered the scene too late? Nana's Aimee Semple McPherson, who famously said she'd rather see her daughter dead than catch her at a dance hall, spent considerable energy insisting municipalities pass laws severely curtailing gambling. So much energy, in fact, that she, and the rest of the Holiness movement, eradicated it from modern evangelicalism the same way that Dr. Jonas Salk eradicated polio from the developed world.

Maybe?

CHAPTER 8

A BRIEF HISTORY OF GAMBLING IN AMERICA

As the modern Indian casinos dotting highways and byways portend, these United States of America had an ancient gambling tradition long predating the arrival of European settlers. Richly varied games, some athletic, some purely games of chance, were wagered on with joyous abandon by Indigenous Americans long before Dostoyevsky but finding similar joy.

According to Lewis Henry Morgan, a mid-1800s anthropologist best known for his work on the Iroquois people, "games were not only played at their religious festivals, but special days were set frequently apart for their celebration. Betting upon the result was common among the Iroquois. As this practice was never reprobated by their religious teachers, but on the contrary, rather encouraged, it frequently led to the most reckless indulgence. It often happened that the Indian gambled away every valuable article which he possessed; his tomahawk, his medal, his ornaments, and even his blanket."

Unlike the buoyant attitude of Iroquois "keepers of the faith"—those who directed religious business in the tribe—toward risk, chance, and good lucky fun, European perspectives toward gambling were decidedly mixed. Lords and ladies were betting on horses as early as the 1500s in England, with the first casino being built in Venice, Italy, in 1638, the most beautiful in Baden-Baden, Germany, in 1824.

The Kurhaus, or spa house, with stately columns and neoclassical grandiosity there on the edge of the Black Forest, is where one of literature's most celebrated risktakers, Fyodor Mikhaylovich Dostoyevsky, hulked around with his rich wife's money in the pocket of his black Russian overcoat, "going into convulsions" at the sound of its jingle. The author loved to gamble so much that he was forced to write a novella in a ridiculously short amount of time in order to pay off his gambling debts.

Dostoyevsky knew the singular, heart-gripping moments that gambling can provide. Knew the soaring heights and crushing lows of placing all hope in the bounce of the ball, or as his protagonist Alexei Ivanovich says in *The Gambler*, "Well, what, what new thing can they say to me that I don't know myself? And is that the point? The point here is that—one turn of the wheel, and everything changes, and these same moralizers will be the first (I'm sure of it) to come with friendly jokes to congratulate me. And they won't all turn away from me as they do now. Spit on them all! What am I now? Zero. What may I be tomorrow? Tomorrow I may rise from the dead and begin to live anew! I may find the man in me before he's lost!"

The Russian Orthodox Church, to which Dostoyevsky belonged, did not believe that gambling allowed a man to rise from the dead and begin to live anew. It held, in fact, that gambling is in complete opposition to God's grace, with Jesus Christ the only one who died for us to begin life anew.

Catholics, on the other hand, were indifferent, even assigning Saint Pantaleon as gambling's patron. The young first-century martyr had come to Christianity by way of his mother but fell away from the faith after she died, becoming a nurse and serving the emperor, Galerius. Later, the Bishop of Nicomedia brought him back into the true Christian fold, and he converted his pagan father, who bestowed upon him a large fortune. After his death—either by beheading, being tossed into a pit with wild animals, dipped in a vat of molten lava, or pitched into the sea with a large boulder tied to his legs, according to the varying accounts—he was said to give gamblers, particularly lotto players, insight into what numbers they should play.

Early Protestants appreciated none of this business, neither the veneration of saints nor Catholics in general, and they, like the Orthodox, especially did not like gambling. By the end of the sixteenth century, the Puritans, Methodists, Wesleyans, and other church reformers felt that life had become far too debaucherously decadent and sought to cook off the bad bits that kept people from properly focusing attention on God. These included dancing, drinking, smoking, carousing, and most certainly gambling. These same Puritans, holding their noses at the rotten stink of moral decline, then sailed to the newly established American colonies, shipping their undesirables to Australia, and directly "ordered that all persons whatsoever that have cards, dice or tables in their houses, shall make away with them before the next court under pain of punishment."

But the Puritans only held sway in certain towns. Outside of those, there were no wide-scale restrictions. Lotteries flourished, funding the building and maintenance of growing towns, and betting the ponies became an obsession in Virginia, where increasingly wealthy landowners codified a system, including how to bet, dress, speak, eat, and drink that kept the dirty, unwashed masses away.

It was a fine move, in retrospect, because if history has taught us anything, it is that gambling looks best either super-crazy rich and unfazed or super-crazy rich and desperate. James Bond playing baccarat with Dr. No in London, playing baccarat with Xenia Onatopp in Monaco, in all of its five-star glory; James Bond playing poker against Le Chiffre in Montenegro.

But it ultimately became a form of middle-class gaming that spread throughout a now-independent nation. Gambling houses popped up in towns dotting the eastern seaboard from north to south. Gambling riverboats chugged down the mighty Mississippi to New Orleans, where French Catholics prayed to their Saint Pantaleon and rolled the dice. Clapboard gambling saloons sprung from the Wild West soil where frontier men, already gambling on precarious fortunes from gold, fur, and cattle, also threw their money down on black, red, or green and held their breath while fortuna spun.

Gambling was, more or less, everywhere until the United States had its own two Great Awakenings, and Baptists, Seventh-day Adventists, Congregationalists, and all manner of Pentecostals came down hard on vice, pounding enough pulpits to outlaw alcohol throughout the country by 1920, and also gambling, by and large. Horse tracks shuttered, card parlors boarded up, riverboats scuttled as Aimee Semple McPherson, young Nana, young Pastor Chuck, and other Americans spent their time at tent revivals.

But just like prohibition didn't stop drinking, outlawing gambling didn't stop people from betting. Just like with booze, it simply drove it into the arms of outlaws, with underground numbers rackets helping to feed organized crime in cities like New York, Chicago, and Kansas City. But enterprising gangsters saw even greater opportunity in a dirty desert town almost all the way out West called fabulous Las Vegas.

The State of Nevada, admitted into the Union in 1864, had legalized gambling in 1934 to little fanfare. Cowboys and military men, stationed at Las Vegas–adjacent bases, parted with their money then went about their business until one Benjamin "Bugsy" Siegel let his imagination run wild.

A New Yorker with connections to both Jewish and Italian-American mobs, Siegel had traveled to southern Nevada in the 1930s in order to provide "illicit services" to men building the Boulder Dam (later renamed Hoover Dam). Realizing Las Vegas's potential as a pit stop on the way to Los Angeles from points east, he soon secured enough capital to build the Flamingo. A gambling palace with great liquor and food, entertainment, and reasonable prices, the Flamingo further cemented America's middle-class gambling tradition.

Mobsters from Chicago and Kansas City joined their New York brethren, and soon the Las Vegas Strip, running through the center of town, was a wonder world of lights, bourgeois glamour, the singsong bells of one-armed bandits taking donations from happy middle-class suburbanites, and Frank Sinatra, Sammy Davis Jr., and Dean Martin crooning sweet nothings.

In the 1970s, Nevada passed laws allowing public corporations to own casinos, which diminished the mob's control and supercharged the development and building of gargantuan Roman, Egyptian, and Parisian replicas all sociologically tuned for massive profit. Elsewhere around the United States, waning heavy-handed morality led to an odd patchwork of state-by-state regulation. Gambling riverboats floated in New Orleans, bingo halls opened in Alabama, and lotteries bloomed almost everywhere, save Utah, and Indian casinos began to dot the highways and byways across these United States.

Though their gambling traditions were, indeed, ancient, the Indian casino did not exist until the late 1970s, for it was then that Russell and Helen Bryan changed history. The married couple belonged to the Chippewa tribe and were living happily in their cozy mobile home on Chippewa land in northern Minnesota. Happily until Russell waltzed to his mailbox one afternoon, per the usual, opened it up, and discovered a property tax bill from the state.

Now, the Bryans had never received a property bill before, and it was quite frustrating, seeing that their people had lived on that land for thousands of years before there was any such thing as a United States of America. Russell refused to pay it.

The case wound up before the state district court, where it was won by the state, before being recontested in the Minnesota Supreme Court, where it was again won by the state, before being kicked all the way up to the United States Supreme Court. There, in a landmark unanimous decision, Chief Justice Brennan declared that not only did states not have the right to tax Indigenous Americans, they didn't have the right to regulate them on their reservations altogether.

Bingo.

The Indian Gaming Regulatory Act, signed into law by president Ronald Reagan in 1988, further allowed Indigenous Americans to build "casino-like halls" on their lands, and here we are today, with vast majority of Indian casinos in California, Arizona, Washington, Minnesota, and Oklahoma, plus a smattering more in twenty-five other states including Connecticut.

While gambling is a wonderful revenue generator for Indigenous American tribes and an enjoyable way to pass a few hours at the Wynn between a gluten-free sweet-and-sour chicken dinner at Wazuzu and tickets to Cirque du Soleil's *Le Rêve*, it is not without peril.

Dostoyevsky had to write *The Gambler* in record time, in between *Crime and Punishment* and *The Idiot*, under severe distress, in order to stay out of jail and/or alive.

The 1974 film *The Gambler*, borrowing the title of Dostoyevsky's masterpiece but not the storyline, followed Axel Freed, played by James Caan, an English professor who taught Dostoyevsky to inspired students and had it all. A loving wife, the respect of his university colleagues, the respect of his successful family, but he couldn't help his compulsion to risk it all on chance. He digs himself into a $44,000 hole blowing basketball bets, borrows money from his doctor mother, blows it again on more basketball bets, then pays a college basketball star, his student, to throw a game so he can win it all back.

In the end he refuses to pay a prostitute, fights her pimp, and gets slashed in the face.

Mark Wahlberg of Marky Mark and the Funky Bunch remade the film forty years later, using the same title, though critics were mixed—Bilge Ebiri of *New York* magazine's *Vulture* wrote,

"Wahlberg grows into the part. He may not be right as a pre-cocious, self-loathing intellectual, but he's very much at home playing a dickhead who's gotten in too deep."

"Getting in too deep," clinically, is now called "problem gambling" and was first included in the American Psychiatric Association's *Diagnostic and Statistical Manual of Mental Disorders* (DSM) in 1980, largely thanks to Dr. Robert L. Custer. Before his work, taking sweaty, seemingly unnecessary risk was seen as a replacement for sex in a classic Freudian overreach. Dr. Custer argued that it was not merely bad behavior but a disease and needed to be treated as such.

Problem gamblers are defined as those whose lives are disrupted or damaged by their gambling behaviors. Destroyed families, careers, lives, etc. The classic sweaty trope pushing all chips in and inevitably losing to a house that inevitably won't. The dopamine rush of going bigger and riskier, Custer had surmised, is pain management gone wild. The afflicted not burning it all down because they hate themselves or are not getting laid but because it feels good in a bad brain.

Problem gambling's carnage is not isolated to the problem gamblers themselves, nor just to their families. Economist and political scientist Dr. Earl Grinols, in his book *Gambling in America*, surmised that those addicted to chance's thrill cost the United States around $54 billion a year—the price of burned savings accounts, college funds, mortgages, businesses, lives.

Casinos, by and large, dutifully warn patrons of the distinct possibility that everything can easily slide into oblivion by posting signs mostly near slot machines that direct people to call Gamblers Anonymous hotlines if they sense annihilation is near.

But it's difficult, if not impossible, to imagine annihilation when sitting in the Mohegan Sun, college debts canceled, financial problems solved, drinks coming from the house, adoring crowd feeling the buzz of the bouncing ball. Difficult, if not impossible, even when a frozen-faced wife is packing a child into the car to go to her parents' house, never to return.

CHAPTER 9

ROB A BANK

It was a swift, relentless fall after Mandi left. Cousin Danny failed both sides of Martin Luther's beautiful edict to "love God and sin boldly," or more accurately in his native German, *Sei ein sünder und lass deine sünden stark sein, aber lass Dein Vertrauen in Christus sei starker.* "Be a sinner, and let your sins be strong, but let your trust in Christ be stronger, [and rejoice in Christ who is the victor over sin, death, and the world]."

The phrase appeared in a letter fragment between Luther and Philip Melanchthon, one of his ardent supporters at the church at Wittenberg, where Luther had nailed his ninety-five theses to the door, thus putting the "protest" in "Protestantism." Luther had run to Wartburg Castle, some 300 kilometers (about 186 miles) to the south and west, in order to avoid execution for his brazen act, but continued to write Melanchthon and others, providing direction to the embryonic movement. How to continue to purify the faith from all manner of rules and regulations, the unnecessary velvet ropes keeping man from his God.

In essence, the letter makes succinct Luther's entire beef with Catholicism. We can never save ourselves no matter how good we try to be, no matter how well we follow the rules and regulations. We are saved by faith alone and that's it. Aimee Semple McPherson knew it. Billy Graham knew it. Chuck Smith and his Jesus People knew it.

Unfortunately, Cousin Danny apparently didn't know it, and officially decided to stop loving God as his burnt marriage turned to ash. Mandi refused to see him, except to drop their young son off for scheduled visitations and retrieve him after, and even then she wouldn't speak to Danny. She filed for divorce. "My misfortune drove me away from spirituality," Cousin Danny said. "I shook my fist at God and told him, 'I'm fucking done with you,' and found every reason not to believe. I looked for distraction now, not understanding. Rebellion felt better than healing."

Except, equally unfortunately, he sinned relatively meekly. The taste of that Connecticut jackpot planted a gambling seed, and he sought to water, fertilize, and grow that high. But again, the Coursons didn't have gambling on the list of capital S-I-N sins. Drinking, yes. Smoking, yes. Surf journalism, apparently.

Gambling, though, not a bold sin. Cousin Danny was hooked and used mathematics and statistics to figure out that he got lucky at the roulette wheel. Very lucky. In roulette, though a wager on red or black might at first seem like 50-50 odds to novices, thanks to the 0 and 00 slots, the odds of winning are only 47.1 percent. Bet enough times and you'll lose everything. So Cousin Danny instead focused on the game he thought he could master.

Blackjack.

He'd study tricks of the trade, applying his collegiate habits, then practice all night at San Diego county's many casinos after silently dropping his young son off with Mandi, eventually venturing into poker too. Looking at the serial gamblers around him and silently judging them as losers and freaks. He wasn't them, wasn't a "problem gambler." He was a winner and gainfully employed.

He'd then head to that job, sleepless, in the morning and get to work in that brightly lit, fastidiously clean operating room. He had settled into total knee replacements and worked on a two-man team alongside an orthopedic surgeon who knocked out four a day. As gambling began to take root, he'd daydream about cards instead of cobalt chromium, titanium, and polyethylene plastic. Cousin Danny's hands bouncing along to a familiar rhythm with his mind in the jacks, kings, queens. He'd begun teaching himself how to count cards and ran through the various options as he sawed bone.

One particular morning, he put a left knee on a right leg as his mind wandered. Now, a left knee can be attached to a right leg, theoretically, but it is like putting a left foot in a right shoe, at least according to Cousin Danny. Works, but not cleanly. Looks bad and feels odd or painful. As he did the final test, pressing the knee down to ensure smooth motion, it instead made a decidedly mundane but extremely loud, clunking sound. The orthopedic surgeon paused, he and Cousin Danny peered into the gap, and they stared at each other.

"Is that what I think it is?" The doctor asked. "What the fuck is in your head?"

Cousin Danny gulped down hard. What could he say? That he had been counting to twenty-one 106 different ways?

The two of them went to work, silently chipping away at the cement, unscrewing the screws—a waste of time, and an embarrassing mistake. Two hours later, they had the left knee on a left leg. Undeterred, Cousin Danny headed straight back to the casino to make it right.

Winning or losing was what felt like something. Winning or losing and riding his brand-new street bike at full throttle up and down San Diego's ample highways and byways. Cousin Danny had coupled his gambling with a full midlife crisis aesthetic, buying not only a motorcycle, but also a throaty sports car. He never specified what bike or sports car; I never saw him in this particular unhinged period, but in my mind, both were Hondas. A CBR-600 and an S2000. Or maybe the bike was a Yamaha YZF-1000 and the car was a Subaru WRX, a sneaky fast production model that could beat a Ferrari off the line, causing much embarrassment to the Ferrari driver, and helping fill the gaping hole of self-worth left in Cousin Danny's heart.

Mornings in the operating room began extremely early and became untenable after late nights at the table, so he asked for more clinic shifts, discussing the procedure with patients before their operations, taking care of patients on their follow-up appointments, making general hospital rounds that he could waltz through with a foggy brain even further consumed by blackjack strategy. He took a pay cut on the nursing side of his work, but blackjack would certainly make up the difference and then some, or to quote James Caan, "I'm not going to lose it. I'm going to gamble it."

He had applied even more of himself to mastering the game. Continuing to learn how to count cards, studying blackjack strategy, memorizing the exact statistical move to make in every situation, blocking out any hunch or instinct.

I'm sure he would have hated to play shoulder to shoulder with me as much as my wife does. Maybe even more, but what's the fun of gambling if the gambler doesn't play hunch and instinct every single time? Where's the gamble? I trust my intuition more than any damned algorithm and so hit when I have thirteen and the dealer is showing seven because my heart is certain that the next card is going to be an eight. Or split when I get two nines because I'm sensing a king, then a queen.

But Cousin Danny learned, then played, the book perfectly, continuing to apply his analytical mind to increase his odds. He'd lose more than he'd win, but the wins intoxicated him, and the online stories he read of card counters, like him, winning millions of dollars kept him upping his risk tolerance.

Soon he didn't care about the win at all, only the risk—only the rush of dopamine fired by going all in. He took out a $26,000 consumer loan from the bank, maxed out six credit cards, sold the sports car, and stopped going to therapy, all in order to save money, all in order to win enough money to climb out of debt. Still didn't consider himself a "problem gambler." He saw them every night. Sat shoulder to shoulder with them. They were losers who had no idea how to game the system, had no apparent jobs, were sweaty, poorly dressed, stuck in the teeth of a totally obvious trap: the alcohol, no windows, no clocks on walls, time being forced to stand still so obvious and silly.

Only affecting those weak wills who get "addicted."

Not affecting a successful, professional Courson like Cousin Danny.

It didn't work.

He slipped deeper and deeper until his rent was late, child support was overdue, and his refrigerator was empty. Life squeezed unbearably tightly all around him. What could he do? How could he solve his problem?

God, having been jettisoned, was not an answer, much less the answer. But what? How? Then one night, alone in his darkened apartment, the answer came to him.

Cousin Danny was going to rob a bank.

He was in his apartment, watching local news like all deadbeat dead-end dads, and a story popped up about an unnamed bank robber who hit a regional branch and made off with an undisclosed sum. The local newscasters, coiffed but aging, bathed in unfortunately white light, clucked their tongues before moving to the next story, but Cousin Danny's analytical mind had fixed on the spare details in the bank robber piece.

The perpetrator had gotten cash. He had gotten away. Nobody was hurt. The government paid back the missing money, so nobody was personally done wrong. He had gotten away. With cash. People hate banks but love bank robbers. Ned Kelly, Jan-Erik Olsson, Jesse James, John Dillinger, Butch Cassidy and the Sundance Kid.

Rob a bank.

Rob a bank.

Rob a bank.

I'm not going to lose it.

I'm going to gamble it.

Rob a bank.

And a wild, unhinged form of redemption. He wasn't loving God, but here, served directly up to him, was a bold sin. A literary, cinematic sin. None of this white picket fence bullshit, purposefully running from an idyllic, albeit boring, suburban life for the thrill of something new. No empty porn, no beer drinking, no gambling. Robbing a bank. Literally, not figuratively, robbing a bank.

Who amongst us has not fantasized about robbing a bank? About busting through the doors with a bold, prepared line like "HANDS TO THE CEILING!" Or, better yet, cribbing from *Pulp Fiction* and screaming, "Any of you fucking pricks move and I'll execute every motherfucking last one of you!" Sure, that line was delivered in a diner, but the sentiment would work and work powerfully, I imagine. Robbing a bank is as American as football, pumpkin pie, Zac Posen, and VH1, and to never have stood in line, waiting to transact, glancing at the wall clock, the inspirational families on posters advertising mortgages, the security cameras, the general daintiness, or youth, of most tellers and thought, "I could take this right now" is to be decidedly un-American.

Cousin Danny needed money and told me very much later that, like Willie Sutton, he too would go where the money was. Sutton was one of the most prolific bank robbers in American history. He stole an estimated $2 million from an unknown, though likely less than Cousin Danny, number of banks during a forty-four-year career, escaping from prison three times for good measure. Once he sculpted an incredibly realistic fake of his own head from plaster, along with a fake of his own hand, replete with human hair and eyelashes, to leave in his bed and trick the guards. The ploy did not work; the head was later valued at an unbelievably low $2,500 on the PBS hit *Antiques Roadshow*.

Sutton's supposed response to "Why do you rob banks?" was: "Because that's where the money is." It became known as "Sutton's Law," which is used in medical school to teach students that the most likely diagnosis is the one that should be chased, as opposed to every single possibility.

Years later he said the journalist made the quote up, further clarifying, "Why did I rob banks? Because I enjoyed it. I loved it.

I was more alive when I was inside a bank, robbing it, than at any other time in my life. I enjoyed everything about it so much that one or two weeks later I'd be out looking for the next job. But to me, the money was the chips, that's all."

Cousin Danny had not had that first taste of the love, the enjoyment, the feeling of being alive yet, but decided it was worth the research. He took his laptop to a nearby coffee shop with free Wi-Fi and began studying.

"I remember making the decision quickly, and making it into a project," he told me later. "Internet searches—sixty-five percent unsolved rate. Okay, not too bad. Legal searches—three years if you get caught without a gun. Okay. But I won't get caught. I will plan. I will execute. I will be clinical, and make this work. No one will know."

Cousin Danny took notes. He dissected successful bank robberies, unsuccessful bank robberies, half-witted, full-witted, every sort of witted in between bank robberies. He made a complete analysis of the science and art of robbing banks including, but not limited to, the Lamm Technique and a study by Italian economists Giovanni Mastrobuoni and David A. Rivers of more than five thousand bank robberies in Italy, the bank robbery capital of Europe. The two wrote the important "Optimizing Criminal Behavior and the Disutility of Prison," which posited an actual equation for who would rob a bank, when and why using $V(t)=[1-Pr(Tp <t)]E[U(W+Y(t),\delta)]+Pr(Tp <t)(W,d,S,\delta)$.

Cousin Danny also studied Carl Gugasian, the "Friday Night Bank Robber," who, like Cousin Danny, had an advanced degree and methodical mind. Gugasian is considered one of the most successful bank robbers in US history, running off a string of at least fifty banks in thirty years, from the early 1970s to the early 2000s, before getting caught. His technique was meticulous, and he stuck to his plan like glue. He operated on the Atlantic northeast coast and would only rob banks on Friday evenings before closing, and only in the autumn or winter, when the sun would set early, casting a melancholy darkness over the land.

He chose banks on the edges of forests and would watch them for many days before hitting. He would hide his plans, getaway maps, weapons, money, clothing, and a bicycle in those forests. His robberies were always under two minutes, and he'd wear baggy clothing to hide his figure and Halloween masks to hide his face, usually Freddy Krueger. Inside the bank he'd move like a cat, able to jump over counters in a single leap, able to carry heavy canvas bags stuffed full of money with ease. He would not use a getaway vehicle but would sprint into the forest and disappear entirely. Miraculously.

The FBI was completely stumped for three decades, until two young boys wandering through a forest near Philadelphia stumbled on a PVC pipe half-buried in a drainage ditch. Curiosity overwhelming them, they pried the cap off one end, dumped out the contents, and entered young boy nirvana.

Five guns, hundreds of bullets, Halloween masks (including Freddy Kreuger), maps of the region, getaway routes, maps to other secret caches, detailed descriptions of banks scattered around the region, and other secret hideouts with fantastic names like "Gnarly Y."

The boys, maybe uninspired, turned it all into local police who, in turn, handed it over to the FBI, who recognized, instantly, that it must belong to the bank robber who had eluded them for so many years.

They set about finding those other caches, most located in Pennsylvania's Poconos, discovered more weapons, makeup kits, cash, climbing gear, and books titled *Ninjutsu: The Art of the Invisible Warrior, The Mystic Arts of the Ninja: Hypnotism, Invisibility and Weaponry,* and a flyer advertising a karate studio in Philadelphia suburb Drexel Hill.

According to the *New York Daily News*, authorities approached the owner of the karate studio, asking if he knew of a very fit middle-age student who might be able to leap very high, possibly over a bank counter, and run very fast.

"Sure," he responded. "Carl Gugasian." Only weeks later, they caught their man entering a library in Philadelphia, the place he had planned many of his heists by using its ample selection of topographical maps. Gugasian confessed immediately, giving up other caches, telling officers how he robbed banks but not why, only saying that he had somehow become stuck into the practice and somehow, inexplicably, couldn't quit.

At his sentencing, he was so overcome with emotion that he was unable to speak, but he offered a written statement reading, "While I have always rationalized my conduct by believing that robbing banks had no victim, I have come to realize that everyone who was forced to endure the harrowing experience of a robbery suffered tremendous harm, even though they were not physically injured."

He was sentenced to seventeen years, and in prison was considered a model prisoner, teaching mathematics to inmates and agreeing to share what he knew about robbing banks with the FBI. He even made a video for the agency in order to help them crack the mad mind. He was released in 2017. Three years later, after a popular podcast featuring his exploits aired, a Reddit user wondered, "So 30 years of bank robbing and 17 years in jail got him something over $2M. Over his 30 years of robbing he averaged about $130K/year robbing banks, or about $85K/year including jail time. Instead, he could've used his masters in systems analysis and gone to Silicon Valley in the early 1970s and become a billionaire."

The first response was, "But he chose to 'work' like 5 hours a year for 130k per."

The logic is difficult to dispute. It did take Gugasian months to work up the nerve to rob his first bank in 1973, though. He chickened out eight times before finally marching up to the teller and making his demand, using his ninja skills, and disappearing into the forest.

It took Cousin Danny one week.

CHAPTER 10

PARADISE FOUND

Cousin Danny hit his first bank in the middle of summer in 2006, near Kearny Mesa, an eastern San Diego suburb with fewer than three thousand residents. It is mostly industrial, featuring dull, flat, one- and two-story buildings, car dealerships, and light manufacturing; it's most famous for its Asian dining options, including conveyor-belt sushi, phenomenal dim sum, and the cutest bubble tea shops. State Route 52 bounds the area to the north, Interstate 805 to the west, and Interstate 15, which goes directly to Las Vegas, to the east.

He had driven his family's nondescript Honda sedan past the bank he had chosen a few times leading up to the robbery, observing traffic patterns, getting a feel for the stoplights, willing the guts it would take to actually *actually* carry it out.

He had circled a Friday on the calendar, just after opening, when it would be flush with cash for those cashing paychecks and those planning weekend getaways. He wasn't alone in selecting the last day of the workweek: Friday has been the most popular day to rob a bank since the FBI started keeping records, with morning being the most popular time, even though Carl Gugasian chose evening.

Cousin Danny didn't sleep the night before, waiting until his chosen time to begin the forty-minute drive, glancing at the commuters driving alongside him, wondering if they knew what he was about to do.

He parked three blocks away, behind a warehouse, on a side street connecting two major thoroughfares that, in turn, connected two major freeways, which connected the rest of Southern California, having learned through his research that it's all about the getaway.

Sitting in the car for a few moments and steadying his pounding heart, he excoriated himself for being insane, for crossing a dangerous line that could land him directly in jail, but then he countered those weak thoughts with Courson panache.

He had this. He was going to win, and solve his problems to boot.

If Cousin Danny hadn't lost his religion, he might have whispered Philippians 4:13 to himself: "I can do all things through Christ, which strengtheneth me." Or maybe Joshua 1:9: "Have not I commanded thee? Be strong and of a good courage; be not afraid, neither be thou dismayed: for the LORD thy God is with thee whithersoever thou goest." He checked his inventory, gleaned from a week of researching bank robbery dos and don'ts.

In a backpack, he had a hammer to be used in case he was locked in the bank and needed to break his way out of glass doors keeping him from freedom; a realistic-looking Glock pellet gun to scare tellers in case things turned bad; a giggle, or boonie, hat, the wide-brimmed chapeau based on the Australian bush hat and used by American military personnel in tropical climates like Vietnam; plus a pair of cheap, wraparound sunglasses from 7-Eleven. He wore a nondescript hooded sweatshirt with another one, in a different color, waiting for him in the backseat.

In his hand he clutched a printed note, in Times New Roman. It had gone through several rewrites the night before, beginning with "GIVE ME ALL THE MONEY AND NOBODY GETS HURT," which he felt was too cliché, transitioning instead to "I HAVE A GUN. NO FUNNY BUSINESS, JUST THE CASH." But he didn't have a gun, at least not a real gun, and also felt silly about using the phrase "funny business." He landed on a final one that felt good, clear, direct: "THIS IS A ROBBERY. 100s, 50s, 20s FROM THE TOP TWO DRAWERS NOW. NO GPS, NO DYE PACKS."

Though he would later forego notes altogether (as they were but another conduit of precious DNA), he was pleased with the final draft, finding it both direct and compelling.

After ten minutes, he donned his boonie hat and sunglasses, staring at himself in his Honda's rearview mirror for a beat or two. He looked ridiculous. He looked *guilty*. But here he was, and the time was now. He clutched his note, swung the door open, left the keys in the ignition, and began the eternal three-block walk to the bank.

"Walk normal," was the only thought pounding in his skull as he put one foot in front of the other. Feeling like he was on an empty, lighted stage with an audience of thousands gazing back at him. He swung his arms the way he thought people were supposed to swing their arms. Kept pace.

Dozens of cars passed down the boulevard, none of them of the cop varietal. He continued, feeling an invisible tug back to his car with each step, pushing through it, moving like molasses until he was in the bank's parking lot and now "TURN AROUND, PSYCHO!" replaced "walk normal" as his only thought, at ten times the volume.

He could smell his own fright.

But he was not turning around and made it to the tinted glass door, pulling it open with the note cupped in his palm to avoid fingerprints. A grandma was on the other side. She smiled, then thanked him, and passed through.

"You're welcome," he replied.

A sign on the door read "Please remove your hat and sunglasses for your safety."

He didn't.

Inside, everything looked dark through his wraparounds and tunnel vision. He saw two people in line and took his spot. Heart pounding. Knowing everyone was looking at him. Feeling the heat of their gaze. His boonie hat felt ridiculous on his head. Like a giant umbrella. Like a neon sign advertising BANK ROBBER.

Now drenched in sweat, the air conditioner was making him shiver.

He could still leave, but also he couldn't. He was a mighty man of God from a long line of mighty men, and before he knew it, he was standing in front of the teller. She didn't know what was coming, didn't ask him to remove his hat and sunglasses, which were now fogging up.

"Can I help you, sir?"

He could make out a blurry smile, but stayed silent and slipped his note to her. As she read, it disappeared. A security camera, directly over her shoulder, blinked. He dipped his head slightly.

Face now clearly terrified, the teller looked at Cousin Danny and then, slowly, reached down, unlocked the drawer, and began deliberately placing stacks of hundreds, fifties, twenties on the counter.

He waited, battling every instinct in his body to grab what was there and flee. Or just plain flee. He stood straight and still, minus the shiver. When she was finished, she took a half step backward. He pulled out a small plastic bag, swept the money off the counter and into it, careful not to touch the counter itself and leave fingerprints, then uttered four words to her:

"Give me the note."

She handed that over too, he put it in the bag, turned, and walked toward the door, bending as he approached so as to mask his height against a measuring tape. Knowing every second was being recorded.

The sun blinded him outside as he broke into an all-out sprint on the way to his car, slicing through the few morning pedestrians. Money tossed on the passenger seat, hat and glasses with it, he smashed the Honda's gas pedal and accidentally peeled out but gained control and, in a flash, was on the 805, having chosen a bank close to the freeway like all the pros suggested, providing easy getaway to everywhere in Southern California, Oregon, or Washington, where he was born, if the spirit so took. Or Las Vegas if he took a quick enough exit back toward the 15. His head was on a swivel as he drove, looking for cop cars, his hand rifling through the bag of cash searching for a GPS device.

Nothing.

Just a pile of money. A pile of solved problems.

Afterward, in his apartment, it took hours to calm down. He tried to watch television, paying particular attention to the news, to see if there was any report of his bank robbery. Flipping among the local channels. There wasn't. He counted his money, totaling nearly $15,000. He drank a glass of whiskey, then two, trying to take the edge off that adrenaline pump. He paced, jumped, felt the fear fade, felt invincible. Felt like he had unlocked a Nietzschean portal where he was above every other dull peon shuffling the earth.

Now, the sensible move, of course, would have been to pay back a hefty portion of his $26,000 consumer loan, stop gambling, pick up extra nursing shifts, continue to dig out of debt while holding the secret of one grand moment—but Cousin Danny was a Courson, and Coursons were superlative.

He was planning his next hit a few days later, having gambled most of his initial haul away, chasing the fading memory of that small fortune won in Connecticut. It didn't work. He needed more money, and that money, as Willie Sutton didn't say, was there in a bank, just waiting for him.

The actual robbery had been remarkably easy, in retrospect, with no real downside. Nobody hurt, nobody but the United States government losing money, and an amount it wouldn't even miss. He had researched, he had carried it out, he had been successful, and he was smarter than all those other desperate fools who got caught. He could do it again. He should do it again.

And so he did do it again. He carefully selected another bank in suburban San Diego, one that was near the dealership where he had purchased his midlife crisis sports car and not too far from the hospital. He spent time observing the comings and goings of customers, observing the security protocols, mapped his routes, and was soon parked behind a shuttered industrial building on a different side street connecting two different major thoroughfares that, in turn, connected three different but equally major freeways. Wearing the same boonie hat and cheap sunglasses. Carrying the same backpack with the same hammer and realistic-looking Glock pellet gun.

He felt a similar gripping panic while walking toward its door, again on Friday, again in the morning, but the screaming consciousness was muted. "TURN AROUND, PSYCHO!" replaced with "turn around, psycho."

A similar pulse opening the door but, even though this was only his second, it felt familiar. That all-too-human ability to normalize and catalog papering over the complete absurdity of his reality.

Cousin Danny marched up to the teller, handed her his note—same phrasing, same wording, same font, different piece of paper. He couldn't discern the look on her face as every fiber of his being was focused on staying calm and maintaining an awareness of his surroundings. Trying to make certain she wasn't putting any GPS trackers on dye packs on the counter between the bills. The damned air-conditioning chilled him to near-freezing once again, and a shiver shot up his spine.

Time stood still. Everything stood still until, finally, the teller backed away from the counter indicating she was finished, Cousin Danny swept it clean into his bag, turned, and walked back out the way he had come in without a sound.

Another pile of cash next to him on the passenger seat, more than he could have earned in a month's nursing. This time he didn't peel out on the getaway but made it, methodically, to the boulevard, then to the freeway. His heart was still pounding, though, and his vision tunneled. Adrenaline coursing through his fibers.

There were no GPS trackers or dye packs, and he made it back home, watched the local news, poured a glass of whiskey, poured another, paced, and willed himself to calm down. This time he felt even better. He was learning, improving, getting better at pacing, control, and command, applying himself to the task. How could he fail? Not only was he better than those desperate fools who got caught, he was better than the high school graduates who went into law enforcement. They didn't have anything close to his intelligence, his clinical approach. They didn't stand a chance. He would beat the banks, the cops, the system over and over and over.

Cousin Danny hit his third bank five days later, this time in south Orange County, just north of San Diego, with even more money, more freeways. A bank robber's paradise. A bank robber's dream. He had spotted it coming home from a visit with his son at a park near his wife's family's home. Her face was cement when she walked him out, eyes darting to his newly purchased sports car, then back to Cousin Danny, burning hot. Taking in his new clothes, haircut, and posture. Some dark aura hovered around him, and she saw he was consumed with sin, unrepentant. She could only imagine the ugly darkness he was getting up to at night. Strip clubs and porn. Drinking.

Little did she know.

The Orange County bank was the easiest yet, mentally and emotionally. He was still completely pinned, but now existed in this extreme state of mind and had also discovered his voice. Handing over printed instructions had worked, initially, but screaming like a manic worked even better. He had learned the trick from further internet research. Humans are remarkably docile creatures, and when screamed at they enter a sort of submissive catatonic state. He was nervous, initially, but once he opened his mouth and let out a gush of expletive-laden instructions, everything worked entirely smoothly.

Life continued normally in the margins—if anything could be considered "normal" anymore. His days were filled with sleepwalking through nursing rounds, rotely explaining upcoming surgical procedures and aftercare best practices to wide-eyed patients. Weekends visiting his son and coaching his son's T-ball team.

Nights were spent gambling in larger and larger amounts. He focused on mastering poker, alongside blackjack, and worked at reading eyes and reactions, knowing when to hold 'em and when to fold 'em, except for all his intensive study, he was losing more and more. He'd head home, empty, when the sun was rising and head back to work while scouting the internet for future target banks, poring over digital maps, plotting his route.

He sped up the pace of those robberies to an unbelievable four banks a week, sometimes two in a day, one before his nursing shift, one after. From the outside, it would have appeared that he was gripped in some sort of manic addiction or he was begging to get caught.

Cousin Danny, though, did not think he was going to get caught. He *knew* he wasn't going to get caught. And with each successful heist, his respect for bank security and for law enforcement shrunk. Nobody was actually invested in slowing his roll. Insurance covered the banks, the tellers were just cashing a paycheck, the police had their hands full with other matters that actually mattered. He was hurting no one, he was solving his immediate problem, and even though the majority of his take was being blackjacked away, he was winning and duplicating his gambling rushes with bank robbery rushes. Rush around the clock. Rush without sleep.

He'd continue watching the local news after each hit and then, one evening, saw himself there. The anchor looking straight at the camera, discussing the spate of bank robberies that had gripped San Diego and Orange Counties. The brazen perpetrator, whose costume of choice was sunglasses and a large boonie hat. He stood there, looking at himself looking at a teller, and felt horror and felt pride.

Famous.

He was famous, or at least infamous, and the anchor described him as "highly intelligent" because he hit so many banks and left so few clues. Described him as a bank-robbing expert—dangerous, no doubt—who was not to be approached. Authorities, the anchor continued, had next to nothing and were asking for the public to call a hotline if they had any information at all.

And manic?

Maybe, but not weird crazy manic. Not need-medication-now manic. An understandable gambler's manic. A oneness with the flow of things. Who would dare step away from the table in the middle of a hot streak? Who would dare leave potential millions behind when the odds had crumbled, when fate had chosen a victor? Each of us has been there, feeling we couldn't lose, and Cousin Danny knew he wasn't going to lose.

He was highly intelligent.

It took him a fraction of the time to knock off nineteen banks that it took Gugasian to knock off his first. Nineteen banks in six weeks, bouncing between San Diego and Orange Counties. A torrid run stretching from to midsummer to early autumn.

Beachgoers and vacationers flocking to the region's beaches none the wiser.

The hot pace may have been misguided, sure, and would not be characterized as "normal" or "healthy" among those who study mental health for their living, but my goodness, isn't the maxim "Do what you do wholeheartedly" not the marker of excellence? A sign of true passion and commitment? Even more so in Christianity of all makes and models, the Apostle Paul instructing the Colossians: "And whatsoever ye do, do it heartily, as to the Lord, and not unto men."

CHAPTER 11

PARADISE LOST

Cousin Danny was ground, heartily, into the pavement, on an on-ramp to the 5 South in Oceanside, California, baseballs bouncing around him, cheek and knees scraping, six weeks after his first bank robbery, on a hot autumn morning, completely surprised.

Utterly baffled.

Not ready for, nor expecting, this.

Police officer screams mingled with other police officer screams, weaving into an incoherent din. The morning sun piercing his eyeballs, the day's heat already rising from the pavement. The officers kept him laying face down, hands tightly handcuffed behind him, while they searched his car for weapons and evidence. Screamed questions—the only one he could make out was about baseballs.

"Why do you have so many baseballs, motherfucker?"

The previous six weeks had been such a surreal blur that being pressed into an on-ramp by screaming police officers didn't necessarily seem strange. Everything was strange. Strange was normal.

Traffic stacked up behind them with commuters craning their necks.

Caught.

He was caught entirely surprised, having pushed that eventuality far out of his mind. But here he was. The pulsing adrenaline, similar to the rush he felt when robbing a bank, allowed him to grit his teeth and stay in the moment. There was no real fear, only moving through each molasses second at a time.

After an eternity, he was hauled into one of the police cars, taken straight to an interrogation room, and kept waiting for hours, the police officers wanting a full confession and no procedural mistakes now that they had their man. The one they had been looking for. They had been mystified by the string of bank robberies, how neat they were and also how rapid their succession. They didn't fit a typical pattern of hardened pro, nor drug-addled yokel, nor sociopathic thrill seeker. Desperation oozed from each hit, but there were no real clues until a partial fingerprint taken from a piece of latex glove revealed their man was a registered nurse named Daniel James Courson. He had taken to wearing latex gloves after that initial robbery in order to conceal his prints, since they had been taken when he enlisted in the Coast Guard. He had no memory of ripping the glove, a dozen robberies in, but had noticed it when he arrived back at his apartment and didn't pay it a second thought.

He was, only to the powers that be, a high-profile criminal who had committed a string of high-profile crimes, and so bail was not offered. He was blasted into another world with its own hierarchies, language, honor, and code. After the initial interrogation, where he refused to speak, he was allowed to see a lawyer, processed, then tossed into a box with no windows and no way to gauge the passing of time save the meals delivered to his cell thrice daily.

But imagine being an evangelical Christian, albeit a former one, from a long line of evangelical Christians, the only one of whom ever breathed prison air being a motorcycle outlaw-in-law with the last name Cool, not Courson. A middle-class, extra-educated officer in the United States Coast Guard, resident assistant of Point Loma Nazarene University, registered nurse. Imagine the complete and utter system shock. Being half of a failed marriage, boozing, observing internet porn, and spending time in gambling halls was one thing. Robbing banks, maybe another, but being locked inside America's industrial prison complex, where there was only wailing and gnashing of teeth—that was something altogether foreign.

"An Astronaut from Planet Vanilla" is how he described himself, finally realizing his childhood dream but going through a decidedly not-NASA route. The reality of his situation hit Cousin Danny. He would not be there for his son, even in a limited capacity. His freedom had evaporated. His not-very-expensive lawyer had told him he was facing a twenty-five-year-stretch. It was enough to convince him to make a break for it.

Before lunch was slid through the door, he had developed a plan and, after rolling it over for a few minutes, told his cellmate that plan. He was going to fake appendicitis and run. His cellmate laughed, then encouraged him.

"Yeah. It'll work."

Cousin Danny talked the nuances out with his now-accomplice for a few hours, then jumped off his bunk and began jogging in place, then adding squats and burpees. Push-ups. Driving his heart rate up, up, up. Sprinting in place. Getting hotter and hotter. Heart rate higher and higher. Then, after thirty minutes, he reached out, pressed the intercom button, and said, "I'm feeling really sick. I need help now."

The annoyed guards came a few moments later, and Cousin Danny explained that his stomach was killing him, that he had raging diarrhea and was burning up with fever. One of them told him to drink some water and lay down.

Cousin Danny grunted that he'd already tried that and it hadn't worked, then burped that he was going to puke and bent over their guard boots. That got them. The other said, "Alright, alright. Come out. We'll walk you down to the infirmary."

He knew he had it, here. Knew his Rutgers training would trump whichever cut-rate doctor was working the San Diego prison system. He was bent over at the waist, writhing in pain, the entire way there.

"Yup, appendicitis. Let's get him to the hospital . . ." the doc said.

Cousin Danny winked, internally, as he was shuttled out, writhing for effect, to the transport van and sent to downtown San Diego to a proper, non-prison hospital and a real emergency room. The van stopped at some creepy back entrance, he was shuttled up the ramp and into a crowded hall, then laid on a gurney with his leg shackled to its metal railing, continuing to writhe in faux pain so he could assess his surroundings. The staff busily rushing. The patients being wheeled in and out. His prospects for escape hampered by his leg shackle and the two guards assigned to his case.

After a few minutes, a pretty, younger doctor came to assess his situation. He had zero guilt lying to the prison doctor and to the guards, but felt a pang lying to one of his own-adjacent. Still, he knew where to grab, knew when to wince, and she promised pain medication would be on the way soon, along with a CT scan. He also knew he needed to act fast. Morphine would provide an unfortunate fuzz on his decision-making skills, but before he could do anything a nurse arrived, plugged an IV into his arm, and filled his body with slow warmth.

Damn it. He willed his mind to focus and was fully aware that one of his two guards had loudly announced he was going to get coffee before shuffling down the hall. This was his chance.

He ratcheted up his bellowing, then began screaming he was going to defecate all over the place to the remaining guard. Finally the guard caved, unlocked him from the railing, and began escorting him toward a nearby bathroom. Pressing for more, Cousin Danny asked that he uncuff him too so that he could writhe in peace. Again, the guard relented, and there Cousin Danny stood, unshackled, uncuffed, outside of prison.

He stared at himself in the mirror for a few moments, willing courage, then just as he willed himself to rob that first bank, he threw open the door, which knocked his guard back, and then was free. Cousin Danny spun and ran down the hall, prison-issue sandals slapping the cold tile, screams all around. He ran toward the entrance, dodging nurses, doctors, and patients, wheelchairs, medical carts, and gurneys, and then was outside, down the creepy ambulance ramp and into downtown San Diego, hearing a commotion behind him, assuming gunshots were forthcoming.

There were no gunshots, though, just footfalls growing louder and louder and louder. He knew he was being chased, and well-chased, but he kept running, trying to sort which way to turn, not having mapped out his escape route like he would have otherwise. Straight or down the alley to the left?

He chose the alley to the left, into a dead end, and realized his mistake directly. But when he spun around, he came face to face with his pursuers who were, surprisingly, not cops, but two young, extremely fit emergency room technicians. He tried to dodge and scoot around them, but they were lightning quick and pounced on him. It was a tangled mess of flesh, and even though Cousin Danny was the one filled to the brim with desperation, he could not break free.

"FREEZE, ASSHOLE!" was the next thing he heard, twisting his neck to look directly down the barrel of a drawn pistol. He was hauled to his feet, cuffed, and shackled, while his guards thanked the EMTs for "helping with the track star."

"Actually, we both ran track at San Diego State . . ." one EMTs responded, laughing even though it was not funny to Cousin Danny. Not at all.

He was taken back to the hospital, paraded down the hall to rounds of mocking applause, forced into the CT scanner, and read the results from a dead-eyed doctor.

No appendicitis.

Months later, after much behind-the-scenes negotiating, Cousin Danny pled guilty and wound up sentenced to an eight-year run. Shockingly lenient. Nineteen banks plus an attempted escape? Still, eight years is a long time, but what could he do except sort out his new, forced lifestyle? "His kind" did not exist behind bars. He was not like the guards, and instantly grew to loathe them and their wielding of unconditional power. He was not like the other inmates and generally looked down on them as "savages," though he found his place in the hierarchy by helping them write letters to their families, providing clarity into the prison library's law books, and stitching up their wounds.

Lucky for him, bank robbers have credibility inside, and so he wasn't pulled into the worst racial warfare, but no one is fully exempt from the law of the jungle. He found himself having to fight every now and again for respect, and had his will slowly drained away, learning, like all inmates, to keep his mind preoccupied on menial tasks, ticking through the day without hoping for anything more than a letter from home or a warm shower.

I remember the first time I heard Cousin Danny was in prison for robbing multiple banks. My mother had called me in early October. The Dow Jones had just hit a record high, Google had announced it would purchase a video sharing website called YouTube for more than one and a half billion dollars, and I had just come back from Lebanon, having covered the 2006 Israeli invasion for Al Gore's television station Current TV with my best friends, Josh and Nate.

Josh and I had been detained by Hezbollah—blindfolded and interrogated. We had almost been bombed and almost taken out by drones, and I felt that I was living up to my Uncle Dave ideal. Taking his Indiana Jones Harrison Ford meets *Mosquito Coast* Harrison Ford but remixing it into *Miss Congeniality* Sandra Bullock meets *Miss Congeniality 2: Armed and Fabulous* Sandra Bullock.

Life was good—great, even—and I was certainly on my way to fame and fortune when my Nokia (the only phone available in the Middle East), featuring Arabic script and numerals on keypad, rang.

"Hi, Mom."

"You might hear about this on the news, but Danny is in jail."

"Nurse Danny?"

"He was arrested a few days ago."

"For what?"

"He might have robbed some banks."

"Nurse Danny might have robbed some banks?"

"Well . . . yes."

She didn't have any other details, though I'm sure my sister was peppering her already to get some, so I immediately hung up and called Emily.

"Did you hear Cousin Danny is in jail for robbing banks?"

"I KNOW!"

My sister loved Courson gossip more than anyone, and though she loved Cousins Danny and Mikey, she nursed a long-standing grudge against Uncle Dave for making her take the bus, once, when she visited him in Oahu, where he had moved after Vanuatu, because he "needed to stay behind at the church and talk to people" after preaching the Calvary Chapel sermon.

The Coursons, famously tight-lipped, kept everything under wraps, but she was an old-school newspaper journalist, and once she smelled a scoop, she would force my mother to get details by calling each of her brothers, making awkward small talk, then doing her best to pry salient nuggets away.

"I told mom she *has* to call Kris right away, and she better call Dave too. Apparently, his roommate turned him in!"

"Nurse Danny had a roommate?"

I had known that his marriage with Mandi was not in the best shape, but evangelicals are never-say-die when it comes to definitively declaring one over, so I had fully assumed that they would work it out.

"YES. His name was James Caputo, and I think he got arrested too. It's in the newspaper!"

That gem, the roommate business, Cousin Danny later told me, was not true. The police had identified Cousin Danny through that partial fingerprint on a latex glove. They had also arrested another bank robbery suspect at the same time, and their cases got mixed up in the press.

I laughed, anyhow, and hard, at Cousin Danny and his alleged snitchy Italian American roommate. Making gentle fun of our family foibles, the proper Courson uniqueness, had become sport for my sister and me, though those early years of utter amazement at the fame hadn't exactly melted away. Uncle Jonny had come to speak at Calvary Chapel Costa Mesa a few times when I was at Biola and once, after a Wednesday night Bible study, he took me, my roommate, and a few friends out to Denny's. I sat at the far end of the table in complete awe as he walked us through Biblical prophecy, laughed his broad laugh, asked us questions about Old Testament specifics. I also semicasually dropped his name when I knew somebody was a Calvary person, just to watch their eyes go wide. The breath get caught in their lungs. I still do, if I'm completely honest, like last week, when I told famous Channel Islands surfboard shaper/owner Britt Merrick. He had difficulty believing it and had to call back the next day to confirm.

"Jon Courson is actually your uncle? Real uncle?"

The Calvary pastors had become superstars, but there were four at the apex. Pastor Chuck at Costa Mesa; Pastor Greg Laurie at Harvest in Riverside, who also headlined the yearly Harvest Crusades, bringing hundreds of thousands to various Southern California stadiums; Pastor Raul Ries in Diamond Bar; and Pastor Jon Courson of Applegate Christian Fellowship.

"Yes." I told Britt. "My mother's younger brother."

Cousin Danny's new reality, in any case, was one part Courson comedy, one part tragedy, one part absolute Hollywood blockbuster. No Courson had ever done anything as purely cool as robbing nineteen banks in a six-week stretch. No Courson had ever destroyed himself so thoroughly, wrenching himself away from a young child who would lose his father for years and years. No Courson had ever done anything so patently absurd, ridiculous.

Cousin Danny. Nurse Danny. The Floppy Hat Bandit. The Boonie Hat Bandit. An American folk hero?

After my sister and I hung up, I thought about him, what he did, where he was throughout the weeks. I had been detained by Hezbollah, thrown into a bloody dungeon, interrogated but freed, and in light of Cousin Danny, my escapades felt half-baked, like a pulled punch, and I pondered our two paths, where we had been, where we were, where we were going.

Nineteen banks in six weeks. An unparalleled achievement. To knock off that many, that quickly, would have taken intense focus, unrelenting preparation, skill, drive, ability, desire. Some overarching motivation that couldn't be sated by one, two, three successful takes. Imagine getting away with ten bank hits successfully. Imagine pushing that beyond ten to eleven, twelve, thirteen.

Why?

Self-sabotage? Some adrenaline disease? Or something I felt intimately myself? Something innately Courson? Never ever being able to back away. Never ever being able to stop if the internal voice rang, "You are being a chicken."

CHAPTER 12

DO NOT WEAR CLOTHING THAT RESEMBLES THE CLOTHING THAT PRISONERS WEAR

Cousin Danny had been locked away for more than two years by the time I finally made it down to visit him at Richard J. Donovan Correctional Facility, that dusty prison overlooking the US-Mexican border.

It was my first time in a prison, and it was surprisingly depressing. I had been prepared for bleak, for soul crushing, for supremely undesirable, but a certain romanticism lingered in the margins of my addled brain. Cool Hand Luke eating eggs and inspiring revolution. Papillon working fantastic schemes and stitching fantastic straw hats. George Clooney in his three best movies ever, *From Dusk Till Dawn*, *O Brother, Where Art Thou?*, and *Out of Sight*, bringing such charisma to being a convict, but the reality was just plain awful.

I'd woken up at first light and rescanned the dress restrictions so as to make sure not to fall afoul. It would have been harsh business to have jumped through all the other hoops—registering, applying, being accepted by both the state of California and Cousin Danny—only to get sent all the way home for a sartorial misstep. The rules, from the California Department of Corrections and Rehabilitation, were lengthy:

1. Do not wear clothing that resembles the clothing that prisoners wear
    a. Blue denim pants;
    b. Blue chambray shirts;
    c. Orange jumpsuits or orange tops with orange bottoms;
    d. Red tops (Pleasant Valley State Prison only); or
    e. Dresses that resemble prisoner muumuu (female institutions only)
2. Do not wear clothing that resembles what custodial staff wear
    a. Forest green pants;
    b. Tan shirts; or
    c. Camouflage
3. Dress conservatively and modestly; and
4. Do not wear any item that cannot be taken off and will not clear a metal detector (such as an underwire bra or clothing with metal buttons).

There are specific restrictions:
- No blue denim, blue chambray, orange jumpsuits or orange tops with orange bottoms;
- No forest green bottoms with tan tops;

- No camouflage unless identification shows active or reserve military personnel;
- No strapless, halter, bare midriff, sheer, or transparent clothing;
- No skirts, dresses, or shorts that expose more than two inches above the knee;
- No clothing that exposes the breast, genitalia, or buttocks area;
- No very tight, form-fitting attire;
- No wigs, hairpieces, extensions, or other headpieces except for medical reasons and with prior approval;
- No hats or gloves, except with prior approval or in inclement weather; and
- No shower shoes.

I looked at the black moccasins I had planned to wear and wondered if they could be considered shower shoes, but otherwise felt safe in my black-on-black decision—and also felt like Johnny Cash might have before performing at San Quentin.

My parents, who were not yet utterly disheartened by my surf journalism life, picked me up from my northeast Los Angeles bungalow and we swung by McDonald's, where I ordered a sausage, egg, and cheese McGriddle, hash browns, and coffee, then pointed south, driving past downtown LA into its gritty industrial south, which blended without distinction into Orange County's industrial north, home to Biola University; Orange County's rich-but-tasteless south; San Diego's yoga-infused north, Cousin Danny's onetime home; and San Diego's dusty south, turning left along the US-Mexico border before arriving at

Richard J. Donovan Correctional Facility, perched on a perfectly depressing mesa.

Three bigger two-story buildings that looked like industrial four-pointed stars nearly touched points on the dead ground with another, longer two-story building running in a straight line to the north. It could not have been more depressing. Prison is, no doubt, punishment, but punishing the aesthetic sense so utterly, so completely, should have been deemed cruel and unusual. There was no hope to be found in the gray concrete walls, no hope in the pallid blue roofs. No hope in the gravel-strewn parking lot, the concertina wire–topped chain-link fencing that warned of the potentially dangerous human cast-offs on its other side, or in the sign, which attempted to mimic the signs of California State Parks but mocked them instead. "Welcome Richard J. Donovan Correctional Facility."

Welcome, indeed.

My father parked, and we got in line with other families who seemed to know exactly what they were doing, boarded a bus that took us onto the actual prison grounds, then got in another line. Not a piece of form-fitting attire in sight, zero green-on-khaki combinations or standard blue denim. My father told me, as we waited to be processed, that prisoners washed their state-issued uniforms in the toilets before visiting day in order to spiff up. He had taught English in various prisons around California after he and my mother fled coastal Oregon's depressing pall a year after my graduation from Marshfield High School, often befriending the inmates, and he knew that visiting day was the only highlight of the month, or year, for many inside.

Eventually we were let into the visiting room, a spartan area with metal tables only knee high bolted to the floor so everything is in plain sight, torturous fluorescent lighting flickering above, jailed vending machines in the corner, and a guard booth stuffed with bored but strong men. The cement, everywhere gray cement, was monotone but polished. Closed-circuit television cameras observing.

A buzz sounded, a thick door opened, and inmates walked through in a straight line. I saw Cousin Danny immediately and he saw us, a smile flickering on his face. He looked every inch the slick con. The lack of nutrition slimming him to perfect, cinematographic scrawn. Push-ups, sit-ups, time in the yard, a few fights defining his physical appearance, aligning it, just right. His hair was slicked back, and his blue-denim uniform was crisp and neat. I wondered if he had washed it in the toilet.

He greeted us with a mix of appreciation and overt shame, eyes broadcasting a profound sadness, mouth attempting a gregarious smile. "Bet you never thought you'd be meeting your old Cousin Danny here," he said while shifting his jaw to the side in that way he did. We sat down at a table. The "old" borrowed straight from Uncle Dave, who always referred to himself as "your old Uncle Dave."

I didn't think he should feel any shame and launched in straight away.

"Are you kidding me? Being a bank robber and convict is so much better than being a nurse! You are living the relative dream."

He laughed, but it was self-deprecating laugh, revealing none of the deep pride he had buried deep inside. None of the distinction he felt from those others dressed the same, at similar tables, talking to their families.

He told us how much he appreciated us coming to see him, being the first of his non-immediate family to do. My father gave him a pep talk on the prisoners he had known who used their time locked up to turn their lives around and serve the Lord in various capacities upon release. Cousin Danny nodded, eyes filling with tears, and spoke softly about how badly he had messed up but how he was in the Word every day, learning from his mistakes, accepting the Lord's ceaseless grace.

He asked after our family, spoke glowingly of how his son was doing, his eyes filling with tears once again, and after I had gone to the vending machine to get us some Chex Mix, he pointed out a few lifers, men who would spend the rest of their days here, or in similar facilities.

"How in the world did you start robbing banks?" I asked him right before our visiting time came to an end. He rubbed his freshly shaved chin and was about to say something when Sirhan Sirhan sauntered past, short and gray with wild eyes, square jaw. A proper footnote in American history, the tautologically named Palestinian.

Robert F. Kennedy had been a virtual lock for the 1968 Democratic presidential nomination before he was gunned down outside the downtown Los Angeles Ambassador Hotel with a .22-caliber revolver. Sports journalist George Plimpton and hard-bitten New York everyman journalist Jimmy Breslin, among others, wrestled the twenty-four-year-old to the ground in the chaotic aftermath. It was considered the first incident of political violence in the United States stemming from the Arab-Israel conflict, as Sirhan's motivation was tied to Kennedy's support of Israel's purchase of American-made fighter jets.

Sirhan was quickly sentenced to death in 1969, but that was commuted to life in 1972, with a possibility for parole. He had just arrived at Donovan, after bouncing around various central California facilities, including the literarily rich San Quentin.

After the distraction, I told Cousin Danny to write. To write every ounce of what he had done, those robberies, those getaways, that thrill, and then those behind bars years too. To spend all those enviable hours with absolutely nothing else to do except write to write, because robbing banks was arguably the coolest thing any Courson had ever done, and certainly cooler than being a nurse.

He laughed and thanked us again for caring enough to pay him a visit. I asked if any other Courson had dawned Donovan's door, or written any letters, and he shook his head no, except Nana, who had written religiously, but he expected his son to visit later that month and was very excited.

And like that I retreated back north to East Los Angeles with my parents. A head full of prison, trying to imagine what Cousin Danny's life looked like, felt like after we left. Did he go back to his cell and scratch another hash mark on the wall? Did he help an inmate with spelling? Continue digging in his cell's wall with a spoon behind a poster of Raquel Welch? Trying to imagine what I would be doing if I was him, besides penning a Pulitzer Prize winner, but also not understanding what drove him down such a bold path to begin with. Damn you, Sirhan Sirhan.

Why hadn't any Coursons come to visit? We had been close, undeniably closer than other extended families I knew, and legendary. More legendary than any I knew except the Prefontaines, who lived a few blocks away in Coos Bay and whose son, Steve, had run track at my Marshfield High School. I didn't know why that made him famous until not one, but two, big screen biopics starring Jared Leto and Billy Crudup respectively told his story.

Imagine being portrayed by two of the most handsome actors of 2005–2010? Either could play Cousin Danny.

So where were Uncles Jonny and Jimmy? Jesus, and the men who took His message throughout the world, were decidedly pro-prisoner. Jesus declared he had come to set the captives free. Saint Peter, upon whom the church was built, Saint Paul, who spread it all to gentiles, Saint Silas, Saint John, Saint James . . . virtually every New Testament character spent time in prison and preached or wrote in prison metaphors. Their letters, or epistles, are filled with captives being set free and chains broken. Of prison guards coming to know the power of Jesus, miraculous escapes and full-blown prison revivals.

Now a Courson was actually in jail, and silence? Why the complete lack of literary appreciation, much less spiritual? A classic Courson sense of privacy? Decorum in not wanting, or presuming, to shame Uncle Dave with his familial circumstances?

An honest mystery, and the only thing that could be ruled out was an inability to stare unfathomable pain directly in the eye. Lest the reader imagine that the Coursons could maintain a veneer of everything being cool, of everything being shipshape, due to a lack of trauma, I'm here, though still a surf journalist, to declare the family suffered a string of misfortunes heavy enough to bring a Russian novelist to his knees.

This was especially true as it related to Uncle Jonny. He had lost his beautiful wife that he had met at Biola in a car crash where he was behind the wheel. He lost his effervescent daughter sixteen years later, on the same winding network of southern Oregon roads. His oldest boy, Old Testament prophet Cousin Petey, developed Crohn's disease in college, then cancer that would eventually end his life right after he turned forty. Grampy died in the hospital after simply hurting his knee mowing the lawn. The doctor mixed the medicine wrong and shot a blood clot to his heart, killing him instantly at an all-too-young sixty-three. None of them ever lingered in pain, but they all certainly felt it, and it shone out of Courson eyes, crinkled at the corners, a retreating blue.

An inability to deal with the deepest pain wasn't what kept the Coursons away, but something certainly did, and I pondered deeply what it could possibly be during the following days. The profoundly depressing smell, sound, look, feel of Donovan's visiting room lingering in the recesses of my mind, trying to stumble upon an answer, until wondering if my literal interpretation of the Biblical prison stories was crooked. That, yes, Jesus had come to set the captives free, but Cousin Danny, even behind bars, wasn't actually a prisoner. He was still unbent. Yes, he may have felt remorsefulish behind bars, away from his son—his tears may be real—but he also maintained that Nietzschean Übermensch archetype.

He wrote me while sitting in prison, staring down the consequences of his actions, staring down bologna sandwiches without mayonnaise, and racial violence:

> Something feels good about making the illogical choice,
> the reckless choice, after a life of a carefully planned
> 401k, a mortgage, a wife, and kid. Being able to say "Fuck
> you," finally, to the universe, underlined by the biggest
> possible consequences, freed me. In my mind, I was
> always right, making the logical, correct choice under the
> circumstances. Everything I was doing, even the robberies,
> was automatically right at that moment of action. Even

when I had a moment of clarity, of honesty, telling myself, "STOP. You're a moron—this is so wrong!" I'm right. I'm right about being wrong. I'm right even when I'm a moron. No matter how impulsively stupid robbing banks and gambling was, I was doomed to be right, because it was mine. I owned it.

No, Cousin Danny had not let his will bend when faced with ruin, both personally and financially. Spiritually. He had stared at his problems directly, unflinchingly, and did not ask for help from God nor family but acted like those mighty men of God before him, except without God, and so simply man, a glorious literary flameout, who had robbed a bank then another then another then another—and what were the other Coursons supposed to do with Nietzsche clothed in a disciple's robe?

CHAPTER 13

NOTHING COULD BE MORE ABSURD THAN MORAL LESSONS AT SUCH A MOMENT

Cousin Danny got out of prison just under eight years after entering. A free glorious literary flameout, Nietzschean man—though as a registered ex-convict that meant no voting, regular visits with a parole officer, and not leaving the state of California. Plus, he was required to cough up that he was an ex-convict on job applications. But still, he was free if not all that mighty.

I had just moved to Cardiff-by-the-Sea, just down the 5 freeway from Cousin Danny's Carlsbad, recently divorced but even more recently remarried, though maybe illegally.

Like many good Christian boys, I had married, right out of Biola, in a haze of well-intentioned holiness. My young wife and I were going to do it right and good and beat the odds. She had had Broadway aspirations when we met, and I was absolutely smitten with her big voice and comedic timing, convinced that her name would one day be in lights.

While she chased Broadway, then film, then television, then commercial work, I chased Islamic radicalism, heading to Yemen, Syria, Lebanon, Azerbaijan, etc. every chance I could wrangle. Writing, filming, surfing, with my two best friends. Exploring the fringes of our burning world. To me, our combination was perfect. We were Madeleine L'Engle (me) and Hugh Franklin (her). A writer/actor couple who lived L'Engle's *Two-Part Invention*, wherein she detailed the various difficulties, but mostly glories, of an artistic union.

My wife didn't feel the same way and became increasingly annoyed with me and my adventures while increasingly disheartened with her own prospects. But movie-quality dreams are why humans live, and I was thrilled at her getting back to Broadway, and thrilled to be chasing more radicalism.

I taught English as a Second Language at Glendale City College, Pasadena City College, Los Angeles City College, and University of Southern California with my applied linguistics degree after realizing Bible translation was a long shot. The work suited me, though I did not suit the work, and I regularly told my students not to tell the administration about the weeks I'd vacate to Somalia and, in return, I'd give them all A grades.

It was all intoxicating, everyone happy, except my wife in New York who continually grumbled that things were not working out and never would. But I was dogmatically attached to a cinematic ideal, an asshole, and stumbled into a way out, blowing the whole thing up with an affair with a Ukrainian blonde, and there I was, like Uncle Dave and Cousin Danny. The third Courson to crash and shamefully burn, but the first Smith.

I wasn't proud of my actions, but not nearly as contrite as I should have been, and quickly fled to Australia on a rocket to surf journalism fame, pushing buttons, causing problems, being a proper jerk. After a year bouncing between Sydney and Melbourne, I came home to direct a surf film, met a famous ex-snowboarder-cum-most powerful agent in extreme sports at a surf film festival, and insisted that she marry me.

She was a native Oregonian too, possessing the same Hessian heart that beat in my chest, and even though I was a surf journalist and she drove a white Porsche 911, she agreed.

Film–esque dreams.

We wed in Las Vegas in front of a raucous crowd of her famous extreme sports clients and my derelict Australian surf journalist friends, less than three months after first meeting, and I moved into her beautiful Cardiff-by-the-Sea home, promising that I would make more money than her in a year because I was going to write a Pulitzer Prize–winning book.

My ex-wife did send a piece of registered mail to my better, new, and last wife in those first weeks declaring that we hadn't been officially divorced before the Las Vegas wedding. She called me a bigamist and included portions of the legal code that forbade bigamy in the United States.

I felt like an almost cool outlaw. A little like Cousin Danny, who had moved back in with his mother, Uncle Dave's first wife, after his release. She still lived in Carlsbad, and we met at a coffee shop overlooking Warm Water Jetty, coming entirely full circle.

Cousin Danny still looked good. The pale musculature of prison was complimented by a Southern California tan, as he was surfing with his son as often as the court and his ex-wife allowed, but there was real frustration floating right behind his blue eyes. A bubbling rage expressing itself in his shifted jaw.

We ordered our coffees, sat at an outside picnic bench, and caught up on old times. Surfing and surf culture, mostly. He was saying the right things, happy to be out, never wanted to go back, was working . . . but the work, at a phone bank trying to sell medical devices to seniors—he was better than that, prouder than that. He spoke disparagingly of his idiotic managers, senile clients, work beneath his expertise. Those clients jawing about whatever garbage they thought they needed and prices being too high and his power-tripping parole officer were all beneath him and blocking his Übermensch way.

Back in his Point Loma Nazarene and grad school days in New Jersey, he was a beach lifeguard and thought that *maybe* he could get back into that, especially since he was now also an ex–Coast Guard officer. It would at least satisfy physically.

He trained and tried out back at his old Warm Water Jetty-adjacent California State Parks stomping grounds, made it through the tryouts, swimming, paddling, and running with a grip of prospects that made him feel unfortunately old, but still beat out enough of them and got to the interview.

"Most supervisors were all new, but there were a few holdouts from my old lifeguarding days," he told me while we sipped our coffee, jaw shifted. "I did the interview, and at the end, I took a deep breath, and came clean about my crimes and prison time, in case they didn't know. I was just trying to be honest. They stared at me, thanked me for my honesty, and I waited. A couple of weeks later, the predicted phone call came. 'Yeah, Dan, thanks so much for your hard work to get in shape and try out, but we can't have convicted felons on the beach. You understand.' I remember that moment being one of the first that I realized my life is fucked, and I will be paying for my shit forever."

But what's a man to do? Especially one who was proud enough not to ask for help when he got into trouble with gambling and decided a better option was to rob banks instead? Not just one or two but nineteen, went to prison, came out but still had that pride fully intact? An Übermensch? Continue calling geriatrics trying to push medical alarms and in-home diaper services?

No.

I saw Cousin Danny once more after that. He had met my first wife and was nonplussed when I told him we were divorced, but was shocked when I told him I got remarried to a woman named Circe Wallace. "Circe Wallace? *The* Circe Wallace? Mike and I have watched all of her snowboarding clips!"

There was a moment, in the mid-nineties, when snowboarding really hit hard amongst surfers. Our way of life had already become mainstream and accepted. Soft and wildly marketable. Snowboarding, on the other hand, was raw, aggressive, mean, and banned on many mountains. We all, Cousins Danny and Mikey very much included, would watch bootlegged copies of snowboard VHSes and envy our chilly brethren and their rock 'n' roll lifestyles.

Cousin Danny and I continued discussing kids, snowboarding, the current job market. I picked his brain more about bank robbing and life in prison because it endlessly fascinated me. Having to toughen up, fight on multiple levels. Mind-torturing boredom but also all the time in the world to write. He asked about Kelly Slater. I told him that the world's most famous surfer was odd. We parted with a hug and promised to get together soon.

A month passed, then two. We texted some, nothing particularly noteworthy. He was still surfing with his son, when he could, struggling under the weight of uninspired work. Then I had to go to Oahu's North Shore for a few weeks to continue my powerful rise in surf journalism, coming home to Cardiff-by-the-Sea, falling into typical family rhythms. Not keeping up with Cousin Danny at all, assuming he had fallen into his own rhythms, until one bright spring morning when I woke up to a text from my sister simply reading "Max Taylor!" Included was a link to a news story detailing the most recent exploits of a "highly intelligent" con man who had been out on parole after robbing nineteen banks in San Diego and Orange counties, befriended a wealthy fine-art collector with a terminal illness, then attempted to steal over a million dollars' worth of paintings and jewels from his home.

Daniel David Courson, the story continued, had been caught in the act by the terminal collector and fled in a stolen Toyota Tacoma pickup truck, only resurfacing in Park City, Utah, giving guitar lessons, driving the same stolen Toyota Tacoma and dating a girl in Salt Lake City while going by the names Max Taylor, Scott E. Taylor, Max Robert Taylor, Mark Pavlik, and Jeremy Penrod.

Police had almost grabbed him there, but he somehow, magically, eluded them, and they warned the public not to approach but to call law enforcement instead, again emphasizing the "highly intelligent" bit.

What?

Max Taylor?

Dating in Salt Lake City?

CHAPTER 14

A BRIEF HISTORY OF FUGITIVES IN AMERICA

Running from the law does not belong to America. It is, rather, as human as our own skin. The very first people to ever waltz the earth, Adam and Eve, went on the lam directly after eating that forbidden fruit. Their son went on the lam after killing his brother, sweet Abel. Abraham, father of nations, went on the lam to Egypt. Moses went on the lam out of Egypt, four hundred years later, after killing a whip-happy Egyptian guard. Etc., etc., and on up to this modern American minute.

America didn't invent the outlaw, no, though the Land of the Free did turn outlaws into proper, transcendent stars. And by "proper" I mean famous with movies, television shows, serialized podcasts, etc. Dillinger, who we've met, played by Johnny Depp. Billy the Kid, played by Kris Kristofferson, Emilio Estevez, Val Kilmer, and Dane DeHaan, among others. OJ Simpson in the back seat of Al Cowlings's white Ford Bronco running from justice in slow motion—with Cuba Gooding Jr. to later play OJ, even though OJ was already famous, and Malcolm-Jamal Warner to play Al Cowlings.

I don't know that it gets better than Theo Huxtable driving OJ Simpson very slowly in front of a phalanx of cop cars except, of course, for Indiana Jones-cum-*Mosquito Coast* Harrison Ford playing Dr. Richard Kimble. The 1993 cinematic version of the television hit *The Fugitive* set the bar for keeping one step ahead of the law through brains, guts, and sheer audacity. Sure, Dr. Richard Kimble was innocent, but Deputy U.S. Marshal Samuel Gerard, brought spectacularly to life by Tommy Lee Jones, didn't know that. Justice, to those sworn to uphold it, is blind, and running from justice strongly suggests guilt.

The lam.

A thrilling expanse where each of the variances of a normal, dull life are heightened to a maximal degree. Where going to the grocery store, trying to get a job, solving the murder of a wife, or going out on Tinder dates are all laden with severe consequence. The phrase "being on the lam" or "going on the lam" has been in America's English vernacular for more than a hundred years, as it relates to running from the law, but its specific etymology is not altogether clear. Some believe it is derived from Old Norse, where the word "lemja" means "to thrash," which altered in the sixteenth century to lam, or "beat soundly." Thus, to head out on the lam meant to escape a good sound thrashing.

Others believe it finds its roots in Victorian England, where the word "lammas," a bastardization of "nammou," which was somehow related to the word "costermonger" or "one who steals fruits and vegetables from an outdoor vendor."

Mark Twain used the word twice—"lamming the lady" in 1855 and "lam like all creation" in 1865—both meaning "to beat."

The world's first private eye, Allan Pinkerton, wrote in his 1886 memoir *Thirty Years a Detective*, "After (a pickpocket) secures the wallet, he will utter the word 'lam!' This means to let the man go and to get out of the way as soon as possible."

Nonsense, certainly, and while Pinkerton might have been an epic detective, he was no applied linguist, and his contribution to language is the worst sort of folk etymology categorized as legitimate. A real semantic knot that will likely never be untangled, but, for our purposes and also our fathers and grandmothers, the definition is clear. "To lam" meant exactly what "being on the lam" means today, i.e., running from the law.

In 1950, the Federal Bureau of Investigation released its very first FBI Ten Most Wanted list featuring the ten most dangerous, or adept, criminals currently at large. Published in the International News Service, this first list was such a sensation that J. Edgar Hoover immediately made it a regular feature. Grisly mug shots of toughs staring down from post office walls, the frisson of danger while buying stamps, was so intoxicating that it led to a television show, *America's Most Wanted*, that became the second-longest-running show in Fox's history, after *The Simpsons*.

The very first fugitive on that sensational list was Thomas James Holden, who had been locked up in the 1920s for robbing mail trains before graduating to banks. He escaped the famous Leavenworth penitentiary after the equally famous George "Machine Gun" Kelly took a guard hostage, though was caught weeks later on a golf course in Kansas City.

After being paroled in 1949, he killed his wife and her two brothers, then fled. Hoover posted his mug shot, a relatively unremarkable photo of Holden in a white button-up shirt looking at the camera with an inscrutable expression, in the International

News Service. He was caught thirteen months later, in Beaverton, Oregon, after the FBI were tipped off by a local man who had seen Holden's unremarkable photo in *The Oregonian*. Holden, then going by the name John McCullough, was working as a plasterer; he died in prison two years after capture.

James Earl Ray was the first fugitive to make it to the list twice. First, he was wanted for the assassination of Martin Luther King Jr. Ray had been spotted fleeing a boarding house across the street from the Lorraine Motel, where King had been gunned down. A package was found there with a rifle and binoculars besotted with Ray's fingerprints. He had made it to Canada, flown to England, and was arrested at Heathrow Airport two months later, when he was attempting to fly to South Africa. Ray initially confessed, but days later recanted, suggesting some grand conspiracy involving a French-Canadian named Raul.

Second, he was wanted for escaping Brushy Mountain State Penitentiary, later made fictionally famous when Hannibal Lecter requested a transfer to it in exchange for information on Wild Bill. Ray was free for three days, but the Most Wanted List did him quickly in; he died twenty years later in a Nashville prison, insisting that he be cremated and his ashes flown to Ireland since he had been so wronged by the United States government.

Billie Austin Bryant is famous for spending the least amount of time on the list. The convicted bank robber had been working in the prison's automobile shop and escaped custody by crashing a car through the prison's fence. Agents sent out an all-points bulletin, quickly racing the description of a maroon Cadillac up the chain, until the FBI had it blasted out on the Ten Most Wanted.

What sort of person gets a maroon Cadillac fixed in a prison? Bryant fled to his wife's apartment, anyhow, in style, shooting and killing two FBI agents who attempted to enter, then fled again, ending up trapped in a neighbor's attic after he was unable to free the latch. The whole mess took two hours from Most Wanted to police custody and a lifetime incarceration.

Victor Manuel Gerena has spent the longest amount of time on the list, first being included in 1984. The Puerto Rican man, described as stoic and dedicated, worked for Wells Fargo in West Hartford, Connecticut, but was also secretly a member of the Boricua Popular Army, a resistance group that sought to free Puerto Rico from the United States's dirty, interfering paw. One September morning, he tied up two coworkers, loaded $7 million into the trunk of his car, and disappeared.

Reports had him going to Mexico, then Havana, where much of the money was deposited and used for various revolutionary projects. It was the largest cash heist at the time, and Gerena is believed to still be in Cuba—but all leads have run cold. He would be sixty-three now, maybe enjoying his retirement years, washing tender ropa vieja down with exquisite rum punches.

Leslie Isben Rogge gets credited with being the first fugitive on the illustrious list who was captured with help of the internet. The Seattle-born man, dubbed "The Gentleman Bank Robber" for his dashing appearance and calm demeanor, robbed more than thirty banks during a twenty-year stretch. He was polite and genteel by all accounts, and the bank managers he robbed spoke highly of him. Once, one of them fainted during the process, and Rogge revived her before fleeing with his haul. Once, one tried to stand in his way as he attempted to flee in his car, and instead of running her over, he hopped a median in reverse, almost dropping his transmission. He was unique in that he consistently went for the vault, and once made a getaway on a sailboat.

As things happen, though, he was eventually captured in Florida, tried and sentenced to thirty-odd years. Being gentlemanly, he bribed a guard while being held in Moscow, Idaho, and went on a six-year run, continuing to rob banks but also going on a fabulous Central American journey, sailing, dancing, enjoying the *pura vida* except that dang internet.

The FBI began posting fugitives online, and poor Leslie Isben Rogge was top of the list. A Guatemalan man enjoying the wonders of Netscape in 1996 recognized Rogge as "Bill Young" from down the street. Guatemalan officials launched a robust manhunt, and Rogge turned himself into the US Embassy, feeling that noose tightening. He was transferred back to the United States and is set to get out of prison, legitimately, in 2048, when he is 108.

Americans, and apparently Guatemalans too, are fascinated with fugitives, both lining the streets and cheering them on when they're in flight, aiding and abetting them when they can, but also turning them in with reckless abandon. Since the FBI began publishing its ten most-wanted, 94 percent have been captured, 31 percent with the public's assistance.

The odds of eluding justice are far worse than the odds of getting away with a bank robbery, but both occupy a similar romanticized rung of American criminality. Even completely unlovable sociopaths like Boston's Whitey Bulger retained an amount of charm, of underdog appeal, on their run from the law. The organized crime family boss and FBI informant was set to be arrested in 1994 but was tipped off and fled all the way across the country to Santa Monica, California, with his mistress. He lived there for fifteen years while the FBI put a $2 million price on his head, second only to Osama bin Laden's, before being turned in by an Icelandic model.

Five years before his arrest, Bulger, loosely fictionalized, was played to the hilt by Jack Nicholson in the Academy Award–winning film *The Departed.* His character says, "When you decide to be something, you can be it. That's what they don't tell you in the church."

Except they do tell you that. Cousin Danny heard it often in sermons covering both Old and New Testaments, and while Cousin Danny maybe wanted to crack the FBI Top Ten Most Wanted, he failed, though he did make Tustin's Top Ten Most Wanted. Tustin, the most perfectly bland town ever crafted in south Orange County, California—which is a feat, considering Aliso Viejo, Irvine, and Laguna Niguel are also in south Orange County. Costco is the fourth largest employer. Rockwell Collins, a subsidiary of Raytheon Technologies, the second largest. An outdoor shopping mall called The Market Place its most definable landmark.

Cousin Danny was smiling broadly in his mug shot—square jaw, close-cropped hair—next to Angel Sanchez Roman, wanted for burglary. Below Nemir Nasri Tashman, wanted for murder for hire. Catercorner from Shadi Jamal Abbasi, wanted for attempted murder. Who knew that Tustin had such an exotic mixture of criminals on the run from the law? On that lam. The netherworld of dreamy hide-and-seek, with proper stakes, odds certainly not in the fugitive's favor, but still, the fugitive maintaining a puncher's chance—and the puncher's chance is pure Americana.

But not a peep from Max Taylor, Scott E. Taylor, Max Robert Taylor, Mark Pavlik, Jeremy Penrod, Cousin Danny.

CHAPTER 15

FATHOMING SECRETS

A year passed, then two. Not a whisper from Cousin Danny, and silence among the rest of the Coursons. No more news reports about the "highly intelligent" criminal eluding capture in another mountain town. Nothing. I was caught up continuing to climb surf journalism, starting an antidepressive surf website called BeachGrit with a thoroughly degraded Australian and brilliant original thinker named Derek Rielly.

I thought about Cousin Danny often, but also spent the lion's share of my time on stories about Kelly Slater's increasing oddness—exacerbating the surf media competition, fistfighting editors on podcasts, regularly making rude fun of them in posted stories. Like, a nonstop absurd barrage from the world's most famous surfer.

Nana, our matriarch, passed away in southern Oregon after suffering a heart attack in 2017, and a small service was held, graveside, at the pocket Jacksonville cemetery where her husband had been buried nearly two decades earlier. The evangelical

Camelot she had dreamed of continued to grow, expand, and glisten, but some of the dukes and duchesses were not flying the standard as well as we might have.

Cousin Mikey had gone mostly AWOL. Cousin Christy was dressing in lots of black, and her husband, Seth, who once confused Nana with his falsetto, was harboring Hollywood hopes. Like, *secular* Hollywood hopes. Cousin Ellie, Uncle Jimmy's youngest, had married a boy who mixed cocktails on Instagram. My brother Andy didn't ever drum in a Christian rock band, but did play lead guitar in a secular one for some time, opening for Dave Matthews. And I was writing surf journalism, "smut" according to my mother, and getting in podcast scuffles, and Cousin Danny was on the lam after attempting an art-and-jewel heist after getting out of jail, after robbing nineteen banks. He had gone to Park City, Utah, before disappearing entirely.

A specter.

A ghost.

Nobody hearing from him. Nobody really caring, which made my sister Emily extraordinarily frustrated, which I completely understood. How was this not the Courson of the decade? Obviously not in the accepted track, but, still, the most famous? She ordered my mother to get some sort of information from someone. Any sort of information, and our mother swallowed hard and got what she could from the best source possible: Uncle Dave theorized that Cousin Danny had been killed by the mafia for gambling debts. An extremely dubious claim, but the only one put forward, semipublicly, and that was that.

Cousin Danny had vanished.

* * *

Cousin Danny was in fact trying, desperately, to vanish, stuffing garbage bags filled with clothes and personal effects into his nondescript silver Toyota Tacoma. Running back up to his apartment, grabbing more garbage bags, sweating profusely. He had just driven like a maniac, a phalanx of cop cars on his tail, after a bank robbery gone wrong. He'd turned into a suburban Boulder neighborhood, hoping beyond hope that the cops wouldn't endanger the lives of young Colorado boys playing catch with their fathers the same way he would.

And he was empty-handed, having pitched the duffel bag holding his take from the window, assuming a GPS transponder must have been slipped in between stacks from the top two drawers that he had specifically ordered. But he had also specifically ordered there be no dye packs and no GPS transponders.

Damned hero unarmed tellers.

Still, it worked. His high-speed getaway miraculously worked, even though he didn't believe in miracles anymore and he had made it to his apartment, but he wasn't safe. He knew that between a solid description of his Tacoma, DNA from the duffel bag holding the bank cash that he flipped out the window, the bicycle he used for his initial getaway (which flipped out of the bed of his truck when he took a speed bump at 75 mph) covered in more DNA, the police would know, then the FBI would know, that Daniel James Courson, a bank-robbing fugitive on the run from the law, was in town. It was time for him to leave, but he also knew that he would confess his true identity to his girlfriend before splitting, which would lead to even more information.

Heart pounding. He had been here before and knew the drill—or knew-ish the drill—as specific circumstances dictate much of the fugitive life, meaning that no two getaways are the same. A year earlier, he had a wonderful spot in Park City, Utah, minutes from Deer Valley, and was living the fugitive dream. Cousin Danny was skiing daily, and almost got to be a ski instructor, except his fake darknet social security number didn't quite work, leading to an awkward call from Deer Valley's human resources department. He was attending après-ski cocktail parties in the homes of wealthy families and teaching their kids guitar lessons, doing their bookkeeping, as a substitute to being a ski instructor as cover. He was riding his mountain bike in the hills, riding his mountain bike away from banks he had just robbed, feeling that elated rush once more. Filling his lungs with thin air and his corrupted soul with hope. Filling his pockets with money. Gambling much of it away.

He had a different girlfriend then, also gleaned from Tinder. Half-Korean, she had been adopted by a Mormon family as a young child, though abandoned the faith of late. They had lived a beautiful romance even after she became aware of his past life, digging into one of his fake identities and learning the truth, but somehow, she didn't turn him in, instead forcing him to attend Gamblers Anonymous meetings in a town entirely owned by the Latter-day Saints.

He went begrudgingly, faking his way through a handful of the twelve steps, then drove to a dystopian town hugging the Utah border on the Nevada side, that harbored the sin that Mormons refused. There were no gaudy high-rises there. No flaming neon art, Grammy-nominated entertainers, surf or turf buffets. West Wendover was a town built for derelicts, seeing as East Wendover remained in Utah and gambling-free, yet Cousin Danny out-derelicted all comers and eventually got escorted out of town after getting caught counting cards at the tables while wearing a costume.

Attempting to get ski instructor jobs in affluent communities with a darknet social security number, driving across borders to count cards in casinos, Tinder dating and getting found out was not what got Cousin Danny back on the FBI's radar that first time, though. No, it was another Toyota Tacoma, this one white, that he had sold to a woman in eastern California. Her call about her suspicion, after seeing on the news a description of the vehicle, and the man that sold it to her, was transferred to Tustin, California.

Detective Ryan Newton answered. He had been working his way through lower-level drug convictions and trying to find deadbeat dads and various missing persons when the call landed on his desk. A serial bank robber who had gotten out of prison, pulled a jewel and art heist in his jurisdiction, then struck out on the lam without a trace until, maybe, now?

Detective Newton drove the two-hundred-some miles to the caller's house and asked her if he could look inside the cab. She complied, and he spent the next hour looking under the floor mats, behind the seats, in the glove box. Nothing. Right before he gave up, he rubbed his hand across the dashboard at the point it touches the windshield and felt something. Felt a slip of paper. He carefully extracted it, and studied what appeared to be a receipt for a money order.

And there it was.

After tracing the number back to Salt Lake City and Cousin Danny's Max Taylor alias, Detective Newton got to work piecing the web of a life together. He found the guitar lesson business along with a few others, the address in Park City, multiple aliases, and even the Salt Lake City girlfriend.

Detective Newton did not waste any time. He flew out to Utah in order to direct the operation and dispatched two SWAT teams, one to Park City and one to Salt Lake. Cousin Danny was as good as his. The run was over. Detective Newton had his man.

Except a bird in the bush is never easily grabbed by a hand. The SWAT team arrived at his Salt Lake City girlfriend's home first and proceeded to grill her for details. The girlfriend's adult daughter happened to be home and called Cousin Danny, who happened to be at a bookkeeping gig in Park City. She told him what was happening. "They're here for you, Max. The FBI, police, and a detective. My mom is hysterical."

Cousin Danny froze for a second, cold sweat licking his forehead, world shattered, but he knew there was no time for inaction, not yet. He sprinted from the office, knockoff Herman Miller Aeron chair twirling in his wake, parked five houses down from his own, and scanned the street.

Quiet.

He waited for a moment, but nothing changed, so he backed into the driveway, ran inside, and began stuffing garbage bags full of clothes and personal effects, only leaving his ski equipment as a "thank-you" and "sorry" for his landlord.

Once packed, he pointed east and drove as calmly and collectedly as he could, cold sweat pooling in his eye sockets. Cousin Danny slipped though the dragnet with five minutes to spare. Detective Newton had ordered every law enforcement agency he could muster to watch the arteries pumping out of Park City and Salt Lake, but they all came up empty. Nothing but thin mountain air. Corrupted soul gone. The only thing left behind, beyond broken hearts, confused guitar students, and bookkeeping clients, was a story in the Mormon organ *Deseret News*.

And now, one year later, he was going to have to do it all again. Another batch of aliases burned. Credit cards, social security numbers, phone numbers, apartment cooked. Burying Scott Hopkins next to Max Taylor, Scott E. Taylor, Max Robert Taylor, Mark Pavlik, and Jeremy Penrod.

Another girlfriend hurt and abandoned.

Unlike his Salt Lake City flame, this one did not know of his former life. Had no idea whatsoever, and thought her new boyfriend was a traveling medical writer with a painful past, something he didn't much like talking about. They shared a love for the outdoors, hikes in the woods, cozy meals cooked at her home, Netflix, and fake-expensive bottles of red wine while the snow fell gently outside.

Cousin Danny had kept up his bank robbing, folding its full-throttle mania into the comfort of suburbia. Folding that into semiregular twenty-four-hour runs at nearby casinos, Nevada being too far away, under the auspices of laundering the money, but still chasing that all-in thrill.

Life was even better than it had been in Utah, and he was completely depressed to see this version set afire. Profoundly depressed to lose this girlfriend who he maybe actually loved, and he felt duty-bound to tell her who he was, what he did, what he had done before their first Tinder date.

What he had continued to do while mumbling about medical writing.

That he had actually been a fugitive on the run from the FBI, problem gambling, robbing banks, and had just almost gotten caught running away from a just-robbed bank.

That the police had too much now, and would find him quickly if he stuck around.

That Scott Hopkins was now dead and, truthfully, never alive in the first place.

Cousin Danny drove the short thirty miles from Boulder to her place in Denver at a measured pace, dreading the impending conversation, knowing that it would take the detectives hours to pull enough information to begin circling in on Scott Hopkins then onto Daniel David Courson.

He pulled up in front of his girlfriend's house, knocked on the door, then opened it, following his usual custom. She came down the stairs in new hiking clothes, happy to see him.

He had her sit down, then didn't waste any time getting to the meat of it. He told her directly that he was a bank-robbing fugitive on the run from the FBI. That he had to leave. That he was sorry.

She didn't believe him, thinking he was making up some elaborate nonsense in order to end the relationship. He told her it was true, and it sunk in while she beat him with her hands. He tried to explain that he did love her even though virtually every word he had uttered over the course of the year had been built on a lie. He told her his real name, then told her he had to leave. She stayed on the couch, buried too.

Cousin Danny knew the police would be tracking his credit cards once they put the aliases to them, so he headed east, purchasing snacks and getting gas at various stops along the way and using the credit cards in order to throw the trail off. In Kansas, he went on a major shopping spree at an outlet mall, Target, a Nike store, Old Navy—maxing out every credit card on running shoes, ski gear, ridiculously cheap chinos, a guitar to replace the one he had left behind that replaced the first one he had left behind, a new iPhone to replace the one he had just stomped on in the parking lot.

Then he turned around and drove back west, stopping at a Starbucks along the way to borrow Wi-Fi and Google himself. And there he was. The story of his still-fresh escape was already live on Denver's Channel 7, the local ABC affiliate, titled "Slippery fugitive from California, Utah suspected of robbing Northglenn bank" and describing the six-foot-one, 185-pound white man with brown and gray hair and blue eyes who was driving a stolen silver four-door Toyota Tacoma TRD with a Utah license plate marked E048HU. Listing every name the man had gone under, including Scott Hopkins but also Adam Scott Hopkins, Max Taylor, Scott E. Taylor, Max Robert Taylor, Mark Pavlik, and Jeremy Penrod.

The story included pictures of his truck and also his visage, which his girlfriend had taken a few weeks prior. One with a salt-and-pepper five o'clock shadow. The other clean-shaven. Both featuring his broad Courson grin, very similar to Grampy. Almost identical to his father's. He knew immediately that she had called the police as soon as he had left. That she had, for sure, been put in contact with Detective Ryan Newton and spilled answers to whatever questions he asked.

He had assumed she would, and so he was neither surprised nor angry, but it still hurt. It all hurt. But it was time to get serious, again, about options, and he knew the only option was to leave the country entirely. The only problem was that legitimate-esque passports were even harder to come by than legitimate-presenting social security numbers on the darknet. And did he really want to leave?

An international life was exotic, potentially, maybe, but Cousin Danny had not done the same runs as his father or even me. No Khyber Pass, no *Mosquito Coast*, no Beirut, no deep Yemen where no FBI would dare travel. Yes, outside of the United States of America was where the closest proximity to freedom was found, but was he ready to take the leap? Could he take the leap? Is there Tinder in Yemen?

A fugitive dead-set on freedom must leave the country. He had enough cash on hand to live well for years in Cambodia, Morocco, his father's Contra Honduras, my deep Yemen, his father's world, but . . . that was his father's world, and he didn't know it for himself.

CHAPTER 16

WEIRD, RIGHT??

I read the email twice, and slowly, on my phone while floating through Legoland California's Fairy Tale Brook, sitting in a giant plastic leaf next to my young daughter, oohing and ahhhing at Lego Aladdin and Genie engaged in some non-Disney tug of war. Legoland California just so happens to be in Carlsbad, minutes from Cousin Danny's childhood home, from the monkey and the lion in the duplex cage, but wow.

Was this really happening?

> Hey Charlie,
>
> This is Dan—yep, it really is. Weird, right?? I do hope you, wife, and daughters are well these days. I think about our prior get-togethers, both in the big house and in Cardiff, and I'm super thankful for your willingness to talk with me, and take time to see how I was.
>
> This is probably shocking for you, hearing from me, but I'll cut to the chase first, then add the incidentals.

As you know, I fucked up really bad, again(!), and
burglarized a guy's house in Tustin. As is usually the
case, the story is far from the news reports—I had been
producing some fake medical documents and reports for
the guy, so he could cash in on a huge insurance policy. I
basically "gave" him cancer, for which he was supposed to
pay me $75,000. He only got partway with my payments,
so I made the brilliant decision to rob his place. He got
home early, as I was literally lifting a big safe with
thousands in gold coins into my truck. I raced away, sans
safe, and two days later he calls me, saying the cops are
coming and I better bail. Prison sucks, so I took the other
option, and chose the fugitive life, which also sucks, but not
as bad as the rest of my life in that dump.

There are lots of stories since that one, from skiing
with millionaires, to fucking in a bathroom of a mansion
at a high-society party, to more bank robberies (one with a
high-speed chase, even!), to making and blowing thousands
at the casinos, to starting my own businesses, to internet
stalking my son, to molly-fueled partying, to darknet
fake documents, getting pulled over by a Nevada cop
(and released, after I tell him I'm a PA, and he responds
by telling me how much he loves his PA who fixed his
knee), trying to remember what name I'm going by now
when meeting someone new, getting scammed for a fake
passport, etc. I'm not proud of any of this shit, but it is a
story, and possibly entertaining to someone out there.

I've been in contact with Mike recently—you probably
know he's going through chemo for lymphoma. I held off
on contacting anyone in the family, or old friends (for their

sake), but I just had to reach out to him to see how he was.
The last I heard from him he was in good spirits, but it's
gotta be tough for him, to say the least. Do you know how
he is? I haven't heard from him in two months . . .

I took some advice you gave me a while back, and I
wrote about my experiences, but unfortunately I had to
run so quickly from Utah that I left my laptop there, and
I recently learned the cops got that laptop and read all
my writings, which must've been a fun day for them. So,
I've finally gotten sort of settled here, and I'm trying to
reproduce everything. I'm a cliche-addled writer, though,
and it reads badly. This sounds fanboy, but I'm a big fan of
the Grit—I've read just about every article you've written
there, and chuckle (almost) every time, including the
piece you wrote about me—hilarious! The comments were
awesome, too—looks like most of those guys are Aussies?
As soon as my identity is established here (and I have a
credit card), I'll be ordering your book—can't wait! It must
be a relief to be done. I also want to see the Lisa Andersen
flick when it comes out.

I'm sure most out there imagine I'm playing some
game, excited by the chase, manic with criminal energy,
but that just isn't the case. Now three years into this, I
know it's only a matter of time before I'm caught, so I
vacillate between a "fuck it" attitude, spending money I
need on stupid shit and meeting women on dating sites
(not to steal from, but just to fuck—although I fell in love a
couple of times), and losing sleep battling paranoia that the
FBI is on its way to my house. It's a super weird existence,
and there are more stories of daily law-enforcement

avoidance and identity creation. Going to Mexico is a bad
idea—still no passport, and less opportunities to make
money down there. Same with Canada. Today I read your
piece about Raimana, and dreamt of working on a boat
at Chopes.

Maybe someday . . .

Just so you know, my motivation for reaching out
to you is purely writing related. I will never ask you for
money, will never ask to meet you or come to your house,
or for any help related to avoiding the cops. I would never
risk getting you in legal trouble. I have used this email
service to contact Mike and old girlfriends, and also use a
different VPN every time, and all messages are encrypted.
If you wanted to correspond with me, I'd advise creating
your own ProtonMail account to use with mine.

So what is my motivation for this message? I'm not
looking for attention, but sure, I am looking for a friend—
it gets lonely out here, this world of lies and deceit with
everyone I meet. One of my girlfriends out here found out
who I was, and still stayed with me for months, god bless
her. She tried to fix me, taking me to Gamblers Anonymous
meetings. But it didn't work. I'm still a gambling addict,
which makes my casino visits exciting, but expensive. Am
I mentally ill? Debatable. Maybe, but not that relevant. I
truly did buy into all the Jesus stuff for a long time, but
am now agnostic, which dovetails well with my current
situation. I have enough self-imposed guilt, I don't need a
God pouring more on me.

I don't know if you'd be interested in my story, but
it's there for you, a big, mixed-up pile of the fugitive life,

which I am not that good at, and you're a real writer, so
that might be a good combo for something interesting and
possibly even sellable. I'd be so embarrassed to send you
my stuff—again, it's so cliche, and I'm trying too hard.
But I need something to do between bank robberies (kinda
joking, but kinda not?!), so any kind of advice would be
much appreciated.

Whatever you decide to do with this message is totally
cool—ignore it, call the cops, call your lawyer—I completely
understand and wouldn't be upset in the slightest. The last
thing I'd ever want to do is get you in trouble. I do know
the cops are trying to find someone to email me with an
embedded photo in the email, which would have metadata
in the pixels, and as soon as I downloaded it, my location
would be revealed, so I won't open anything with photos,
just FYI. And, you just don't seem like the type who would
turn me in. That may be due partly to your amazingly
awesome podcast incident, fighting with that Inertia
dude, defending your family's honor, and disgust with
his decision to file a police report. What a douche! That is
podcast gold, my friend.

I hope the Smiths are all well these days—I wish I
realized earlier that your branch of the family was always
the coolest. Any news about the fam would be much
appreciated. Thanks for reading, and take care.

Dan

I read the email again.

Incredible.

My daughter asked for another lap on the Fairy Tale Brook.

"Already there, bro . . ." I told her.

Absolutely incredible. A wild missive straight from the lam—it all felt decidedly and profoundly adventurous. Completely unexpected. Dangerous, even, unlike a push fight with a generally lovable, chubby boy from Florida's panhandle with a penchant for calling the cops. I sat back, staring at my cracked iPhone screen for a long minute, wheels spinning, Lego Three Little Pigs dancing a slow jig while a Lego Big Bad Wolf huffed and puffed non-Disney air. Oh how my mind spun, trying to sort how I could leave my family responsibilities behind, for a moment, and join Cousin Danny on the lam. To experience that lam first-person, and how illegal that would actually be. What does aiding and abetting cover? What does "abetting" even mean?

Though I didn't have the hard-nosed journalistic integrity of my sister, I was a sort of journalist and did have an unquenchable appetite for adventure. Finding Cousin Danny, telling his story, describing the way his wild life felt in real time, writing every pulse of adrenaline, every spike in heartrate would be . . . epic.

Where *was* he?

No Courson that I had heard of ever ventured to Utah, where the FBI claimed to have almost scooped him up a year ago, but the family did have a strong tie to bold adventuring in the mountains. Nana's cousin on her mother's side, Art Gilkey, had been part of the storied 1953 American expedition to K2. Young Uncle Dave used to summer on his Cousin Art's Oregon family farm, before the K2 expedition, breathing that cold open air and learning everything he could about the way of adventure. And Old Uncle Dave was currently organizing a trip to summit Mt. Everest with a group of lepers. Literal lepers, suffering from leprosy, the skin-chewing disease made famous in the Bible. In Nepal, lepers are severe outcasts, chased from their families and forced to live lives of immense shame. Uncle Dave figured if he could summit Everest with them, it would prove their worth, even making them heroes like those who climb the Holy Mother.

Skiing in Park City while teaching guitar lessons was hardly akin to legendary attempts on K2 or climbing Everest with lepers, but skiing in Park City while on the run from the law for attempting to steal jewels and art while attempting the near-record in bank robbery was close. Was Cousin Danny still in the Wasatch mountains? The Rockies? Grand Tetons? Had he fled east? Out of the country entirely?

Certainly he was alive and well enough to listen to surf podcasts, but the email held no clues. No geographical hints or flavors. He had been in Utah, that's all I knew. I read his email for a third time before responding, "Your ears must have been burning, boy . . . I think about you all the time. About how you're doing, where you are, how you're feeling, etc. So thank you for reaching out, and tell me more!"

I drove home after playing tag on Castle Hill, buying apple French fries, watching the Heartlake City live show, marched into the kitchen, poured a vodka lemonade, and let my mind race through California's prison system, its parole system, then out beyond its reach. To the lam. A magical land where all things were possible and every mundane movement carried with it the frisson of tension.

What must it feel like to occupy that space daily? To be a bank robber, art-and-jewel thief, on the run from the law and occupying that space daily? Oh man. Oh my goodness. Adventure, of course, but so grand in scope as to be difficult to process.

Cousin Danny had hit the trifecta of awesome. The superfecta, even. Banks, art, jewels, fugitive life. My mind reeled, absolutely reeled, and I went to bed boozed and jealous.

My cousin was cooler than me.

The next morning, I woke up bright and early, stumbled downstairs, and wrote "Help: My Cousin Is Cooler than Me!" on BeachGrit, wondering, "Is there someone in your family whose star shines so much brighter than your own? Who steals the air from the reunion when they walk in? Who throws everything you've tried to accomplish in your life into sharp relief? There is someone in mine. My slightly older cousin, and his name is Dan Courson."

That out of my system, I found ProtonMail, the communication service created by scientists who had met at Organisation Européenne pour la Recherche Nucléaire in Geneva. It was all too easy—username, password, *et voilà*—and now here I was like Indiana Jones at the mouth of a Peruvian cave, Allie Fox docking in Belize City, James Bond sneaking into Goldfinger's lair, Uncle Dave standing next to a laden donkey and two men who were dressed the same as him holding impressive rifles in some snowy moonscape. Uncle Dave doing a training run on Naya Kanga, in the Himalayas, with his lepers.

I was ready for this. For something bigger than life.

I had so many questions, but began with, "Are the fugitive life options sort of amazing? Like, could you start some new religion a la the Rajneesh? Could you easily disappear into some second-amendment-loving West Virginia militia? Could you . . . I don't know . . . what's the fugitive dream? What's your fugitive dream? Have any Coursons reached out to you? What do you think of them now? Are you expecting to get nabbed, or do you think you can dance through eternity . . . or at least death? And please tell me you won't eat a bunch of pills if the heat is closing in. Don't suicide. I love you!"

He responded within hours:

> You hear the same quote, when these guys are caught
> after years living on the lam, "It's a relief this is over—
> I just couldn't take it anymore." The temptation to end the
> loneliness, the paranoia, can be overwhelming. But then
> I remind myself of the terrors of prison, and the resolve to
> stay hidden returns. Fortunately, staying hidden is easier
> for a guy like me. White, no tattoos, unremarkable, easy
> to blend in to the "aging dad trying to look cool" crowd.
> I have zero ex-con vibe going out, which helps me in that
> most important part of meeting someone new—trust. I am
> trusted as harmless, mellow, even a bit cool, but just nerdy
> enough, residing in that zone of "typical."
>
> I tell whatever my story might be for a new town in
> a friendly, laconic manner, interviewing to rent a room or
> for a cash job with a casual air. The discoveries of me as a
> fugitive have come at my own hand.
>
> The fugitive life . . . let's see . . . so far I'm not really
> a fan, as it is a constant struggle to figure out what's next,
> and wondering how close the cops really are. Today driving
> around, a local PD car was behind me for a while, and I'm
> still in my truck (not stolen, by the way), which is a stupid
> move, but fortunately it's a common-looking vehicle, and
> for now, I'm not on the radar of every small PD wanted
> list. Apparently, I'm Tustin's most wanted, though—Tustin,
> ha! My real fugitive dream would be to find an identity, a

quiet location, that will hold up over time, and allow me to live out my life in peace.

I did get word from Mike that Nana had died, and kudos to you for heading to the funeral. It must've been quite dramatic, I'm sure. I bought into the Pollyanna Calvary Chapel/Courson thing for a long time, and basically did my best to bury all the normal struggles that I had as a human, understanding that my dad, the church, Jon, etc., expected all others around them to just be blissed out on Jesus, and that would fix everything. I studied some Calvary Chapel Bible College materials in the pen, and slowly began to realize that so much of it was manipulation of people looking for a cure for their pain.

Maybe it helps some people cope, which is great, but I see a bit of cult-like tendencies there, especially with Jon's church and how he's bringing along Ben and Peter-John [Petey] in the family business. I don't think my dad and the Coursons quite knew what to do with me when my criminal activities began, and instead of being supportive, they basically just ignored me. I didn't fit the preconceived picture of the uber-happy Christian boy anymore, and neither did Mike, and neither did you, so out we went. What're your thoughts about them? I think I can guess . . .

Of course I don't want to get caught, but there's a good chance it will happen eventually. I still take chances, and it's tough for me to sit still in the house all day, so I try to live some sort of life. I go on dates, I did a ton of skiing in Utah, mountain biking, etc., and try and figure out how to make some money. Usually that means robbing another bank, but I have actually gotten to the point where

I am sick of gambling—the ups and downs can be brutal.
Initially I was mostly doing it to launder the bank cash,
but the addiction has been there for a few years now,
and I'd have a lot more cash now if I didn't keep going.
I was even going to Gamblers Anonymous meetings in
Salt Lake City—yep, doing the twelve-step thing, and the
"anonymous" thing helped my situation, but it never really
took, and I was back at the tables soon after that stretch,
seeking another fix.

Ha, no, I've got no plans to off myself if the cops
come a-callin'. I don't even have the guts to point a gun
at somebody else, let alone myself, or swallow a bottle of
pills. Does the loneliness, anxiety, the lies, and fight against
paranoia feel overwhelming? Yep, but all I can do is keep
going, or give up, right? So, onward with this insanity.

At the end of a day, I see it as one more day of
freedom and life, vs. locked in a box, and I actually feel
thankful for that. I know, it's such a weird way to exist,
and I'm not happy for the pain I've caused my son, my
mom, my brother (I sure wish I could be there for him
now), and others, but my options are few, and I've made
my choices.

Be careful who you tell—the cops are looking for
somebody to get to me, and I would hate for them to
pester you. I hope I answered your questions, and please
keep firing them my way. I just don't want you to get in
some kind of trouble. Although, I think you'd fare better
in prison than I did, fighting wise. You have a good reach,
some tattoos, and you could make friends, like I did,
writing for savages.

> Also, I could hear some serious scuffling and neck-
> grabbing on your podcast battle royale—holy shit that was
> so awesome! Ha, in spite of all the great discussions you
> guys have on there (highly entertaining).

There are no great discussions on a surf podcast. I was sad that Cousin Danny didn't think I fit the preconceived picture of the über-happy Christian boy anymore, that he was boiling Courson greatness down to cheap, and in my mind incorrect, "cult-like tendencies." But otherwise I was elated for a real-time view of life on the lam. I could feel the paranoia seeping through. The mania mixed with fatalism. I pictured him in a Starbucks, somewhere nondescript. A Denny's maybe. Mountains? I hoped mountains, yet there were no clues, and I was wary about asking directly, as I didn't entirely trust the French-speaking Swiss with their ability to encrypt.

CHAPTER 17

CAN I POSSIBLY NOT UNDERSTAND MYSELF THAT I AM A LOST MAN?

Oh shit—you made a bank robbery reference in the
podcast! Welcome to the dark side, brother!

Cousin Danny wrote me a few weeks after that initial email. Welcome, indeed. We emailed back and forth almost daily, and bank robbery was virtually all I thought about now. Certainly when driving past a bank and scanning escape routes. Overwhelmingly when inside a bank, very consciously casing it. Feeling like, to fully understand, I would have to do it myself, and to not do it myself was to be a chicken. Being or feeling like a chicken is something I cannot abide. I profoundly understand Marty McFly's reaction to being called a "chicken" in each of the *Back to the Futures*.

I am not a chicken.

But I could never do it, could never do that to my wife and daughters. Could never put myself in a position to be jailed and have them be sad because I had to prove to myself that I wasn't a chicken, therefore making me an even greater one. So I fantasized about some confluence of events that could force me to rob a bank. Like, somehow my wife gets in real trouble with the mafia and needs $20,000 in a handful of hours or else they would cut off her baby toe.

Unlike me, my wife actually made money and had great credit, so it was difficult to create a believable scenario, but that didn't stop me from trying. Maybe our daughters get kidnapped by the mafia when she is overseas, and I have to take matters into my own hands, though I knew my wife would easily sort that out, even from overseas. She's a problem solver.

While I sorted possibilities, I peppered Cousin Danny for impressions of what the whole experience really and truly felt like. I asked him to craft his very best description of a bank robbery.

> Here's the response from everyone I've encountered in the bank: first, frozen, wide-eyed, disbelief. I forget that people aren't used to a masked robber yelling. Then, they slowly comply with whatever I am telling them to do. I used to use a note, but I found it's quicker to just vocalize my demands, and less chance a teller will try and keep the note, or I drop it, etc. I wear sunglasses to hide my eyes, but I am usually breathing hard and sweating, so they fog up a lot. This lends to an even "foggier" memory of what I am seeing. I could honestly never give you a description of what the inside of the banks looked like—I have no memory of anything, other than what was right in front of me. I try and use slightly different disguises, and always toss the clothing I'm wearing.

I have a hammer in my bag, or duct taped to my leg, in case a teller locks me in the bank, so I can break the glass door and escape. I really try and go in only when all customers have left, but a few times there were unexpected customers inside. They either freeze or run out.

I just assume the alarm is pushed right when I walk in, so I never try and stop them, or tell them to give me their cells—I have an internal clock going, and whatever happens, I'm out in 90 seconds tops. I have a police scanner in my car and am monitoring the response when I'm driving away. I usually see cop cars going the opposite direction when I'm driving away, but I know they don't have a vehicle description, so I just drive normally.

As I'm driving away, I am pawing through the money on the passenger seat, looking for a tracking device. If a semi pulls up next to me, I have a sheet I throw over the money. I pull off the freeway three or four miles away to do a more thorough check, then just drive home, go inside, and count it up.

Over the next two days I am constantly checking news reports, to see what kind of photos they got of me. The earlier the photos are posted, I know the less additional information they have. Then I lay low for a few days, driving almost never, just in case they do get a description or photo of my car, which they have a couple of times, from a hidden CCTV camera I didn't see at my parking spot.

The run (or bike ride) to the car is nerve-racking. I go fast, but not all out, which draws attention. Also, I remove my mask, just a guy out for a brisk run/ride. I choose

days with weather that's cool enough to warrant some
extra clothing. With all this planning, though, anything can
happen. Off-duty cop in the bank. Patrol happens to drive
by the bank. Hero customer packing heat. I've read about
all of these scenarios. It's a dangerous game, and not the
smartest crime to commit. The anxiety I feel on a robbery
day, waking up thinking there's a decent chance I'll be
locked up that night, can get intense. A few times I've
aborted a robbery, because something wasn't right, and it's
a relief. It takes me a couple of days to calm down after a
robbery, too.

Hero customer packing heat seemed like an unnecessary flourish
even though it is true the United States of America has the most
guns per capita, even more than Yemen, Serbia, and the Falkland
Islands. I don't know that I've ever read an account of an armed
customer in line at the time of a bank robbery saving the day, but
who was I to criticize?

A damned chicken.

A full-on chicken.

I also needed to know how the lam really and truly felt. Every
bit of that magic.

Every time I go out, I am aware of cops. It helps a lot that
I look "normal," and I've never been looked at twice by
cops walking around. Story: I took my truck into a Jiffy
Lube in Colorado for an oil change a few days after a bank
robbery there. I was sitting in the little waiting room,
when in walked an FBI agent, getting his car serviced.
He had a blue polo shirt on with big FBI lettering on the

front, and in smaller letters, "Rocky Mountain Safe Streets Task Force," the sub-organization that was investigating my robberies.

He sat down a few seats from me, and we sipped our coffees, looking at our phones. I willed my heart rate down, keeping my head down under my ball cap, and didn't look at the guy. By sheer luck, his car was done before mine, because I feared the clerk would call out my name first. I watched the agent get in his car and leave, and finally exhaled.

I took one of my girlfriends to Vegas after a big win at a Colorado casino. We drove there, checked into a nice hotel, and decided to go to a club. When we got to the door after waiting, the bouncer pulled me aside.

"Why the fuck do you have a fake ID?"

Uh-oh.

I had heard that Vegas bouncers are the best in the world at spotting fake IDs, but mine were really, really good, so I decided to risk it. But they caught it, using an upgraded box scanner that I had never seen before. I had a backup story that I had preplanned.

"OK man, check it out—I'm married, but this isn't my wife, so I use this ID when I meet her in Vegas. Can you give me a break?"

He looked at me and her, grinned, handed the ID back, and said, "Get out of here."

Ah, Vegas.

A smarter fugitive would lay a lot lower than I do, but I just lose my mind sitting in the house all the time, so I take these trips, meet people, etc., and try and have a life.

It might get me busted, yes, but I'm willing to take some risk for some fun and a life.

Do I feel at home anywhere? Not inland. Carlsbad will always be home. I loved Point Loma, too. I should probably start heading farther east—more bank-robbing opportunities, less people with concealed guns, but I just hate the east. The mountains were great—Boulder is amazing and utopian—I'm so bummed I had to leave there. But, I've had some fun times in the mountains, and just try and be thankful for what I got to experience. Maybe eventually I can get back.

Oh, the great mountains. Between Cousin Art Gilkey, Uncle Dave, Uncle Jonny in the shadows of Mt. Ashland, and Cousin Danny, I was seriously reconsidering my perpetually coastal life. Damned surfing and the wayward path down which it has led me. The mountains were where I belonged. Genetically where I was supposed to be, which is probably why I convinced an ex-professional snowboarder to marry me even though she, unfortunately, also made too much money for me to rob a bank. Maybe the mafia would take her as well, so she couldn't solve the problem and I'd have a handful of hours to get that $20,000 to save both my wife and my daughters. Oh my goodness, how I'd rob that bank. I'd rob it so amazingly that I'd be entered into the annals of bank-robbing history after just two, since I'd have to rob more than one to get $20,000, per Cousin Danny's calculations. Going after the vault, where the real money is, was time consuming, which made it dangerous. Hitting tellers was quick, but the money was also inconsistent. Sometimes there were tens of thousands in the front of the house. Sometimes only thousands. Speed and the getaway were tantamount, though, if a bank robber wanted to stay free.

But also, the darknet. How in the world does one darknet?

OK, darknet. I'm certainly no expert, but here's how you get started. Do a Google search for "download TOR browser." TOR is basically a browser that allows you to search anonymously, hiding your IP address, thus your physical location. The darknet sites will only allow access if you are using the TOR browser.

Once you download TOR, you are free to access the darknet sites. When you open TOR, it will take you to a search engine called "DuckDuckGo." On the search bar there, just enter "darknet markets," and you will find several options.

Darknet markets are basically just like amazon or eBay, but they sell drugs, fake documents, guides on how to commit crimes, counterfeit stuff, etc., but mostly drugs. They are constantly being monitored and shut down by the Feds (you will never get in trouble just looking at the markets).

The most famous was Silk Road, which was the first big one, shut down a couple of years ago—the main guy tracked down and doing decades in prison. His story is really interesting, his name is something like Ross Ulbricht, just look up Silk Road, you'll find him.

So, after searching for darknet markets, a good site is deepdotweb.com. (You can get to this site just using your regular Chrome or whatever browser, but you can't get to the actual markets, unless you're using TOR.) Click that one, and a list of markets will come up. Click on a link for one, then you will need to create an account name and password, then you're free to shop! I use AlphaBay and Dream Market. All transactions use bitcoin. Let me know if you are able to get on and take a look.

In a few days, I'm moving to a different house, where I can get to most places via my bike, so that will reduce some driving anxiety. I deliberately choose college towns to live in, one reason being there are a lot of out-of-state plates around from students, so mine doesn't stick out.

Sometimes I wonder if the cops are onto me, and every person that walks into this coffee shop, or parks in the parking lot, I give a quick once-over, wondering if they're an undercover Fed. It's a bit paranoid, but it's tough not to wonder. I had a few tough days a month ago, while two local cop vehicles were parked two houses down from mine, and stayed there for a couple of days. I wouldn't say that I let the paranoia get the best of me. I get out every day, and walk around freely, but that thought is always there, and my heart rate shoots up if a cop walks by me on a sidewalk or pulls up behind my car.

This has made me aware of how much we are filmed on camera—most public places. I spot CCTV cameras seemingly everywhere. Facial recognition software is being used in other countries, and it's only a matter of time before it's used here. I was hiking this last weekend with someone, and she took some photos of us, so now I'm worried she'll post them on Facebook, although she doesn't use it much, but still—I can't really say, "Don't take my picture."

When I'm asked why I'm not on social media, my
standard story is that I went through a nasty divorce, shit
got posted on social media sites, so I swore off all that.
People buy it. But all it takes is one friend to put things
together from my photo.

I immediately followed Cousin Danny's instructions and was soon
motoring around an internet that felt decidedly Commodore 64.
Strange, simple fonts, no flashy fun. Stripped down to the very
bare basics, and Cousin Danny was right. Many drugs for sale,
guns, and fake IDs. I wondered how he knew which vendors were
trustworthy? Or does the phrase "honor among thieves" truly
reflect how life is lived outside the law? Between sorting out bitcoin prices, combing the message boards to see who is doing good
work, who has been arrested with computers taken into federal
custody and mined for data, who refuses to produce as quickly as
advertised, who stiffs entirely—the darknet felt like a full-time
job, with sinful booby traps lurking around every pixelated corner.

A rough place for nice boys.

Ross Ulbricht, who created Silk Road, had been a nice boy
like Cousin Danny before his turn to the darknet side. Eagle
Scout, full academic scholarship to the University of Texas at
Dallas, a graduate degree in material sciences with an emphasis
in crystallography at Penn State, but there, in State College, he
took a hard libertarian turn and, after graduating, created his
Silk Road, "an economic simulation to give people a firsthand
experience of what it would be like to live in a world without the
systemic use of force."

Both buyers and sellers were anonymous, using Tor brows-
ers and bitcoin to buy tennis shoes or drugs, hire hitmen get fake

IDs, but this "economic simulation" where freedom reigned was not appreciated by the United States government. They tracked Ulbricht to San Francisco by connecting him to the moniker that he used on Silk Road, Dread Pirate Roberts, distracted him while he sat in the blandest public library among San Francisco's twenty-seven branches, and swiped his computer before he could cleanse it. They nabbed him, flew him to New York, and ordered him held without bail.

Ulbricht's trial lasted just over one month. He was charged with money laundering, conspiracy to commit computer hacking, and conspiracy to traffic narcotics. Convicted on all counts, he was handed a sentence of double life imprisonment plus forty years, without the possibility of parole. More than sixteen times Cousin Danny's sentence for robbing nineteen banks.

It seemed as if poking around on the darknet was as adventurous as anything a man could do, penalty-wise, and so I pressed for more information and, also, needed to know why Cousin Danny chose such bland fake names like Max Taylor, Scott E. Taylor, Max Robert Taylor, Mark Pavlik, Jeremy Penrod, and Scott Hopkins. Imagine being a fugitive and getting to rename yourself at will. I'd throw everyone off and stay Charles Smith, as I already get cockeyed looks from hotel desk clerks and florists. "Okay . . . Charles Smith . . ."

> For me, it's all been trial and error on the darknet. A lot of the "vendors" on there are scammers, as I found out the hard way trying to get a passport. You just have to pick the best one you can tell, from reviews and length on the sites, and go with it. I've never ordered drugs on there, but

you would definitely need a mail drop not linked to you, to go that route.

I have gotten my IDs on websites, not on the darknet. There are a few Chinese manufacturers out there who cater to college kids for underage drinking IDs, and I use those, since everything is done overseas.

The quality is remarkably good, but not foolproof. There was just a huge sting of the most famous fake ID guy, code named Ted Danzig, who ended up being this postdoc engineer on the east coast who had like five million in bitcoin in his little house. I almost ordered from him a couple of years ago—his quality was legendary—but I'm glad I didn't! There used to be a subreddit called FakeIDs that would get me started to fake ID producers, but the subreddit has since been shut down. Like I said, don't buy anything on those sketchy darknet markets—there are Feds lurking. But, if you find a vendor that looks trustworthy, have at it.

I would love to just randomly choose my name— remember Anthony Weiner's? Carlos Danger, I think? Ha! I figured out how to research kids who died, born around my year, born and died in different states, whose name, DOB, SSNs I can use. These allow me to eventually get credit cards after initially getting prepaid cards, and within six months I have a good credit score.

It doesn't work for jobs, though, or trying to convert it into a legit DL. I've tried both, and failed. I also get fake SS cards made, from a forger I found on the darknet, and fake car insurance, registrations, etc. Again, it all won't hold up against a database check, but the forgeries pass initial checks, and have got me out of jams a couple of times. It is almost impossible to get new info inputted into all the government databases (like passports).

No honor among thieves, as it turns out, and no cool names either, unless actually being born a Weiner. The more I poked around on the darknet, the more it seemed like a drug-addled nerd-fest, and I soon grew tired of it. By and large, the world without the systemic use of force is occupied by people with silly, juvenile tastes. Not what I wanted nor cared about, and so gently tried to shift our conversation back to the art of bank robbery.

> I've been thinking "in this box" for a while now, and your questions have been great, but if you have any criminal tendencies that can find life vicariously through me, bring 'em on!
>
> If I was planning another bank job, it would be fun to share that process with you. But that could get you in legal trouble (very tiny chance), so I'll just keep the details of any possible plans to myself, if you don't mind.

"Vicariously through me" stung like a wasp. Like being called "chicken." Like being a chicken. The worst pain. I swallowed hard, gripping the zinc kitchen countertop where I sat reading. Bottles of organic olive oil mocking me. Bottles of Bragg Apple Cider Vinegar with "The Mother" really mocking me. Doing everything I could to stop myself from running out the door, down the street, into the corner Chase Bank, and whispering "This is a robbery" to the first teller who would have me.

The getaway scenario was not good. One street clogged with adults who recently decided surfing was a healthy lifestyle choice, having just enjoyed surfing Cardiff-by-the-Sea's friendly reefs, to one freeway, the 5, heading only north and south. But Cousin Danny had already done the research. A 65 percent unsolved rate. I'd roll those dice any day of the week. So why wasn't I rolling them? Why was I being mocked by bottles filled with healthy salad dressing ingredients?

"Vicariously through me" stung all that night, and worse in the morning, when I went out to interview a surfboard shaper who was well known for his conservative politics, about his new surfboard volume calculator.

Ugh.

How could I get to Cousin Danny? I tried to ferret out clues. Since he was now a fugitive bank robber who had crossed state lines, could he end up in a swanky prison instead of a California hell hole?

Ha, white collar "club med" prisons. Yes, they do exist, but I'll never see one—my felonies are considered violent. Those places are minimum-level federal correctional institutions (FCI). Martha Stewart went to one. I might get prosecuted eventually by the Feds instead of CA or CO, but I would go to a higher level Federal Penitentiary. Those aren't quite as bad as CA prisons (considered the worst living conditions and most violent in the country), but still oppressive, dark, and scary. I talked to a few guys in prison who had done Fed time, and they said the food is a bit better, but there's still violence, gangs, etc.

Status is everything in jail and prison. Accidentally, I had it. When someone would identify me from the news (all criminals love the local crime reports), my celebrity status would be announced. Next I'd be reluctantly holding court, answering every conceivable question from idiots about how to get away with so many bank robberies. Everyone finds their place on the pecking order, some trying to hide their desperate acts of petty thefts, others walking the yard with pride about their destructive accomplishments.

I met interesting people in prison. Kent became a good friend, a double murderer at age 17, now 51, smart enough to be a Google coder, but is stuck typing reports for guards. On an actual typewriter. He showed me the ropes.

I hung out with Bob, a Fortune 500 executive, who killed his wife. He wrangled two years of freedom after his conviction before turning himself in, so he made the most of his money and time. He went on match.com and fucked a lot of clueless gold diggers before ending up on the front page of the San Francisco Examiner: "ONLINE DATING NIGHTMARES."

You don't get to choose a cellmate, which can be problematic. Heroin addicts, Neo-Nazis, meth tweakers and Jesus freaks shared my 9 x 5 foot space. Most became friends. One I fought for my life with.

Prison's code is dominated by race. One day I was playing basketball on the yard, and I got in a fight with a humongous, mentally unstable Mexican named Shadow. The "fight" was more like a couple of glancing blows, but immediately a tribunal is convened to discuss my punishment for fighting another race.

The verdict: Get jumped by two white guys and beat to a bloody pulp.

The beating continued well after I hit the ground, in a fetal position, alarms blaring, cops running toward us, batons smashing into my assailants. I'm whisked to the hole by the cops, and am blessed with some alone time. In a few days, I saw daylight again, only to face the administration.

You're supposed to work in prison. Rehabilitation, they call it. I was assigned a job in the law library as a clerk. Over a few years, I studied the law, and provided free legal service to the fellas who need it. A sustaining purpose to my existence developed, replacing suspicion for the law with some basic understanding, and some small victories kept it interesting.

The biggest victory is my own . . . after being beaten by a jail deputy and needing surgery, I filed a civil suit in federal court, and took it to trial. Bank robber as plaintiff, jail deputy as defendant.

Backwards.

The prison visiting room is a fascinating place. It all happens there: love and hate, sex and drugs, children and parents, hope and despair. Families and friends are treated barely better than inmates. We obsessed a little about visits, and many hours were spent in careful preparation. Ironing, haircuts, smuggled cologne, and fake happiness were all on display.

It was a long walk from the demilitarized zone of the visiting room back to the jungle.

After eight years, I'm given an envelope stuffed with $200 and shown the door.

Rehabilitated.

201

My family hugged me, but nobody cried. They weren't quite sure who I was and if they should worry. We went to get a juicy hamburger, but I couldn't eat it all after years of slop.

I stayed with my mom and her husband in their retirement community, and the parole officer told me how relaxing it was for him to come visit me and the old folks. I got a job as a telemarketer. No background checks. It felt more criminal than robbing banks, convincing naïve small business owners that they needed a new credit-card machine.

The guy in the cubicle next to me has some familiar tats, so one day I glance around, lean over and whisper to him, "When did you get out?"

Fascinating. I couldn't help but be fascinated, even vicariously. I immediately responded with a question about the fight in the cell. About if he had been pressured or forced to join a prison gang. If the prisoners as a whole acted to fight the guards. I couldn't wait to hear back.

Except I didn't. One day, two days, three days—and all of a sudden it sunk in that Cousin Danny was really actually wanted by the FBI, various local law enforcement, and Tustin's finest. This all just wasn't a fun game of hide-and-seek.

CHAPTER 18

A NICE PLACE
FOR ROUGH BOYS

Cousin Danny stood in his bathroom staring into the mirror, wondering if he could pull it off. Not a return back to his Courson roots, exactly, but nearer Pastor Jon Courson than bank robber John Dillinger. He didn't look the part, he didn't sound the part, but "hippies in trees" were more a part of his heritage than scaring bank tellers, and mustering that overall feel could be the thing that would save him from a life always looking over his shoulder.

His hair wasn't right. His eyes weren't right, nor his talking points. He'd have to invent a backstory, but he'd have a long two-day drive on which to come up with one convincing enough to explain his clean-cuttedness. Why he needed to be part of an "intentional community."

Cousin Danny hadn't spent all his internet time just communicating with me. He was a busy fugitive, perpetually trying to figure out how to stay out of the claws of justice, planning routes around banks, buying fake IDs with uninspired though necessary names, online dating, and researching places where he could disappear. This was how he had stumbled on a commune in rural Virginia.

Twin Oaks looked interesting enough. Founded in 1967 and built on an old tobacco farm in Virginia, the community had wanted to be a utopian society, but squabbling about which behaviors were actually "utopian" led to abandonment of ideals and an embrace of egalitarian work principles.

It had grown, over the years, and now allows one hundred members who each work forty-two-hour work weeks either in a tofu factory, making hammocks, or taking care of the children. In return, everything is free, from room to food to entertainment. Prospective members usually have to wait a few months for a space to open up and then are invited to come to the property for a three-week tryout, after which the existing members vote them in or out.

Cousin Danny was not excited about "living intentionally" with "hippies," but the membership, decided only by existing members with no background checks, was appealing, so he emailed the director and put his name on the list. After a few months, she invited him for his three-week tryout.

Now, if Cousin Danny could just develop a backstory as to why a middle-age, clean-cut white male was suddenly making such a drastic life change, he might be able to hide for the rest of his days, living in "peace" while making tofu for forty-two damned hours a week.

After brushing his teeth and steeling himself, he left his small apartment and began driving east in his bank robbery getaway truck with fake license plates, fake registration, and a fake driver's license. All of it would work, at first glance, but if a cop decided to run any of them, his luck would instantly run dry. He was paranoid, and cursed his lack of preparation here, but also felt that if he just drove the speed limit and didn't do anything stupid, he'd be okay.

He was right, and two days later, Cousin Danny drove off the small Virginia State Route 697 and down the small dirt road leading to Twin Oaks. The nearest small town, population 1,555, was thirty minutes away. Richmond a farther forty-eight, but Richmond is hardly a major metropolitan center. Thick trees surrounded him. Bugs committed a suicidal barrage against his windshield. Through their guts, he saw a farmhouse that he recognized from the internet. A handful of people wearing wide-brimmed sunhats and overalls were bent over nearby, plucking something from the dirt or planting something.

Cousin Danny parked at the road's end, opened his door, and walked as confidently as he could, even though the summer humidity pressed against his West Coast–now–mountain sensibilities. Even though the forest had strange trees, and strange bugs buzzed and hissed through the air.

There was an old clapboard house that had a sign reading "Welcome to Twin Oaks" nailed above its dilapidated screened doorway.

Inside, a small knot of visitors (he presumed) were standing around a wooden counter listening to a middle-age woman named Kim who sported a long skirt and a longer ponytail. She seemed friendly enough, and he swallowed the bile rising up and stood among the noobs for a moment before she recognized his entrance.

"Adam? I'm presuming this is Adam, and it's so great to have you here."

She smiled broadly, showcasing teeth that rejected fluoride toothpaste and the whitening agents it generally employed.

"Adam"—which should have been a symbolic name choice based on the first man ever mentioned in the Bible but was merely plucked from the list of dead kids born in Cousin Danny's same year—introduced himself to the institutionalized hippie in front of him as well as his fellow applicants. I feel like he should have been frustrated with yet another bummer name, though it was the very least of his worries. Getting locked into an extended question/answer session with any of them was the most, so he nodded, half-smiled, and said the absolute minimum of what he needed to say. "Nice to meet you. Nice to finally be here."

He was twice their age and clean cut. They were not choosing the intentional community life in order to hide from art-and-jewel thefts plus multiple bank robberies and the FBI. They were choosing it because they actually believed in the egalitarian lifestyle.

Kim led them on a quick tour of the grounds. The tofu factory. The hammock making. She explained the history and the bikes that were free for residents to borrow and the old bike shop that fixed them freely too, then said, "Dinner's at six; have a look around, and we'll see you then."

Cousin Danny recoiled as the true, or at least true-adjacent, applicants milled around and split from the group as soon as it was appropriate to "explore" by himself. He clearly was not like any of the others. Too old. Too normal-looking. Not idealistic enough. He was having a difficult time mustering even a passable wide eye. He didn't want to get in any drawn-out conversations about who he was and what he was doing, so found his way to the homemade swimming pond that had been cut from the loamy, nicotine-infused earth a decade or so earlier.

It was hot, so hot. His mind raced with what he had just experienced. Kids running barefoot here and there. Tofu. Could he do it? Could he assimilate? If he could somehow sort out his aesthetic revulsion, it meant that he would, theoretically, never see the inside of a jail cell again, though he may well have to share a bathroom with someone who believed in communal living. If he couldn't, it was back to the heavy fugitive life. Perpetually looking over shoulder. Never comfortable.

The lake was small, inviting, but also occupied. Two nude women were sunning themselves on a dock in the middle. Not sure what the etiquette was, not sure if this was a women's-only hour.

He called out, "Uh—hello—is it okay if I swim here?"

They both laughed, "Visitor, huh? Come on in!"

Cousin Danny decided he would have to interact, at some point, and it was extremely hot. So he stripped his clothes off and slunk into the water.

"Come over to the dock!" They shouted. "We won't bite."

He slowly breaststroked out, seeing they were both tan all over, very unlike his complete paleness, and that one looked slightly older than he was, with the other looking slightly younger.

When he arrived, he overenthusiastically complimented the water temperature as a way to stay in it, but they weren't buying.

"Come up here."

He hoisted himself up, embarrassed.

"So what do you know about us?" The slightly older one asked. She had spiky blond hair and world-weary eyes.

He told them only what he had read online and what Kim had just briefly shared.

That made her laugh for some reason.

"What do you know about polyamory?" She asked.

"Oh, not too much . . ." Cousin Danny answered, feeling off and creepy—and more creepy when the slightly younger one pulled herself up, brushed the hair out of her eyes, shot him a look, and said, "Bye . . ." before diving into the water and swimming to shore.

The slightly older one continued, undaunted, explaining that nearly all the members of the community swapped partners fairly regularly, and that this sometimes led to hurt feelings and jealousy. She told him, briefly, what brought her to Twin Oaks and what she liked about it, though she didn't deliver the last bit with much conviction.

Cousin Danny listened politely, thanked her for the chat, told her it was nice to meet her, and said he wanted to do a bit more swimming before heading back, slipping into the water without waiting for her response.

After treading a wide lap around the lake's diameter, looking up at the dense trees, he returned to where his clothes were piled on the homemade beach, got dressed, and made his way to the guest bunkhouse where he'd be spending the night. He changed, then headed to the main dining hall, walking slow, observing, trying to fit himself into the surroundings.

All meals were eaten together, served buffet-style, and all meals were vegetarian. Even still, the food tasted good, and Cousin Danny listened to the hum of conversation around him. It was a mixture of earnest questions from potential members, earnest answers from existing members, and mundane talk about tofu.

When dinner was finished, the visitors were ushered into the meeting hall, where a large carpeted sinkhole dominated the center. A not-so-subtle nod to the 1960s conversation pit where communal living was discussed with untainted relish. A few of the members joined, curious to get a better look at their potential life partners.

Kim was in front, this time joined by two other women with equally long skirts and longer ponytails leading the lightly mixed bag of young neo-hippies and older idealists in a get-to-know-you session. Each visitor ticked at least one of five boxes: environmentalist, sustainable community enthusiast, socialist idealist, living-off-the-grid weirdo, or, not surprisingly anymore, polyamorist.

Cousin Danny's turn came too soon, and he cleared his throat, ready to roll out the story he had crafted on the two-day drive.

"My world was turned upside-down when I lost my wife, son, job, and religion in the span of six months . . ." he began, leaving out gambling, robbing banks, going to jail, stealing jewels and art, going on the lam, robbing more banks. ". . . I'm here to look for a simpler existence. To be part of a whole that will allow me to wander, spiritually." He looked around the sinkhole and saw nods of approval, understanding in eyes.

Later that evening, as Cousin Danny lay looking at the bottom of the upper bunk, his mind ran through its possibilities. He could live here, for sure. He could figure out how to play the semigenuine seeker role he'd auditioned. But did he want to? He felt certain that the FBI wouldn't find him. That he would blend into the dilapidated woodwork and be gone. But he didn't want to. Continuing to look at the bottom of the upper bunk, it dawned on him that it felt like jail. The intentional community felt like jail, and he'd risk real jail for restaurants, skiing, online dating, spending bank robbery dollars on things other than hammocks and tofu.

The next morning, he left before dawn without saying good-bye. The drive west felt good. Better than the drive east.

He didn't worry about the police or the FBI.

He was free.

CHAPTER 19

INTENTIONAL LIVING

I spent those five silent days not knowing that Cousin Danny was trying to hide by living intentionally, really kicking myself for not figuring out where he was, where he had gone, assuming that I would never hear from him again. Feeling that I had lost my opportunity to hear more about what really drove him from the church pew to standing over a shaky teller demanding that they fill his plastic bag with twenties, fifties, hundreds from the top two drawers with no GPS transponders and no dye packs. Forgetting if he asked for tens or if the United States even produced ten-dollar bills anymore.

To witness life on the lam and . . . maybe rob a bank? I hadn't given up on sorting a narrative that would morally necessitate it. Wife loses job, children starving and/or needing Fortnite accounts refilled, surf journalist only one able to fix? Wife needs to drastically change her appearance suddenly in order to save her life. Like, *really* drastically change it because, maybe, mafia pressure—and can't use her credit cards and also needs cash on hand FAST.

Oh, to have the principled superiority, the clarity of vision, that John Wojtowicz must have had pushing open a Chase Manhattan Bank's glass door, likely already warm from the searing summer heat, white V-neck T-shirt clinging to his stomach. To have the moral high ground when marching up to the teller and slipping her a note reading, "This is an offer you can't refuse."

Wojtowicz's robbery, later depicted by Al Pacino in *Dog Day Afternoon*, is considered one of the most famous in bank-robbing history, and it all began when his unofficial wife, a trans woman named Liz Eden (who had been born Ernie Aron), tried to commit suicide because she couldn't afford to have gender reassignment surgery. Wojitowicz had been married previously to Carmen Bifulco and had two children, but love is love, and, inspired, Wojtowicz set out to solve the financial trouble the same way Cousin Danny sought to solve his own: by robbing a bank. He recruited two friends, Robert Westenberg and Salvatore Naturile, and they drove around Brooklyn on August 22, 1972, looking for a target.

The first one they chose had to be abandoned when one of the three dropped a shotgun. It went off, and they had to flee. The second also had to be abandoned, when Westenberg bumped into one of his mother's friends.

The trio decided to regroup by watching *The Godfather* at a cooled theater, then decided to take the Chase Bank in nearby Gravesend. The note Wojtowicz handed to the teller was a slight riff on Marlon Brando's signature line from the film.

Things went well enough at first, with the three managing to get $38,000 in cash and $170,000 in traveler's checks before an employee was able to alert the police. And then an otherwise semisuccessful bank robbery turned into one of the most famous in history.

The police surrounded the bank. Wojtowicz would dance in and out, telling them what to do while ordering pizza for the eight customers they now had as hostages. The police activity drew attention from the neighborhood, and soon two thousand people were surrounding the bank too, cheering, boozing, otherwise carrying on. A journalist there, watching the scene unfold, described it thusly: "That was a Brooklyn crowd that night." Local television began carrying the story live, national television followed suit, and soon the entire United States of America was glued to the saga.

Wojtowicz played beautifully for the audience, paying the pizza delivery men in wads of bank money, heading back out and throwing more bank money into the cheering night, V-neck T-shirt then really clinging to stomach.

The tellers even grew fond of him, and not in a Stockholm syndrome sort of way, either. They saw themselves in him. Their own middle-class struggles, their dreams unfulfilled because of a perpetual shortage of cash on hand. One said, "I realized that he was friendly . . . had a purpose for robbing the bank . . . he thought he would be in and out."

It took fourteen hours.

Fourteen long, sweaty, insane hours before the FBI agreed to send a car that would take Wojtowicz and Naturile to John F. Kennedy Airport and put them on an international flight (Westenberg had fled before the cops ever arrived). At the airport, things continued to go sideways, as the FBI had zero intention of letting the two escape to a non-extraditable paradise where they'd toast rum drinks while shopping for the world's greatest gender reassignment surgeon.

Naturile was killed in the ensuing shootout, and Wojtowicz was slapped with a twenty-year sentence, of which he served five. "Love is very strange thing," he told Federal Judge Anthony J. Travia. "Some people feel it more deeply than others. I loved my wife, Carmen, I love my son, my daughter, my mother, and love Ernie. Ernie is very, very important to me, and I'd do anything to save him."

Wojtowicz was later paid $7,500 for the story by the producers of *Dog Day Afternoon* and gave the money to Eden for surgery, fulfilling his original intention, then lived a mostly pathetic life, describing himself, glibly, as a pervert and getting arrested for various petty crimes.

Still, August 22, 1972, is a day that will forever live in infamy, and the righteousness of the cause was entirely enviable. Amidst my dreaming of an equally righteous reason to rob a bank, I wondered if Cousin Danny was in the middle of another robbery himself, if he had been laid low in a hail of hero-armed-customer bullets, run off the road in a high-speed chase, discovered wherever he was hiding, shackled, tossed in an armored bus, and driven all the way back to Irvine to be locked in a secret cell underneath a BJ's Restaurant and Brewhouse. The mystery haunted my days.

There was so much more I wanted to ask, so much more I needed to know. I cursed my lack of will in setting out to find him. Cursed my lack of imagination in sorting my own reason to rob a bank.

"Do you need surgery?" I asked my wife.

"No, and if I did, I have insurance," she responded.

Damn it.

Then, as quickly as he had vanished, Cousin Danny was back, via encrypted Swiss email.

> What's your cocktail of choice these days? I've gone back to cheap whiskey on the rocks. Effective, simple, soothing, and makes me feel manly.

"Hmmmm . . ." I responded. "I'm pretty exclusive with vodka soda. In Denmark they call them skinny bitches."

He told me that he had been offline exploring a commune as a possible place to disappear but wrote that it left him unsatisfied.

> Even though it was a commune, everyone seemed to be doing their own thing—there was Wi-Fi and laptops there, and the same device-driven self-isolation in the real world had taken root there. The community dinners were OK— a lot of tofu, no meat, fresh veggies, and again, I was surprised that the residents were really not that friendly, keeping to themselves. Not that my real purpose for being there was to make friends, but the vibe was just too odd, the place is really run-down, bordering on poverty, like a post-apocalyptic summer camp. I just couldn't do it, so I drove back cross country.

And I could only think Cousin Danny hadn't spent enough real time around hippies what with his Carlsbad upbringing. Growing up in Coos Bay, Oregon, with Eugene being the nearest big town, exposed me at a very young age to a virulent hippie strain.

Selling devil sticks in Rastafarian colorways at the outdoor Saturday market. Eating lentils. Shopping for lentils in health food stores wearing baggy, flowy linen pants, leaving a wake of patchouli in a Dead Head wake. But still, I wondered if Cousin Danny had made a miscalculation. While certainly off-putting, hippies develop their own sort of charm with enough exposure, and I couldn't imagine their overall vibe being worse than that of prison guards.

But what did I know? Maybe prison guards were sneakily alluring. I asked him about the cross-country drive, knowing how much paranoia I carried when driving with long-expired tags and/or unpaid parking tickets and/or unattended divorce court hearings. Seeing cops everywhere. Feeling their eyes even when I couldn't see them.

> Driving is anxiety producing. I keep more watch on my rearview mirror than I do out the windshield. I drive like a grandpa, patiently suffering honking speeders behind me. I am always aware of the speed limit, and check my truck's taillights and turn signals once a week. Cops are now routinely using license plate scanners, small boxes mounted on rear fenders that automatically scan every plate the car passes.
>
> I have no ability to register a vehicle (my DLs are all fake), so I buy used license plates on eBay, steal a registration sticker from a parked car, and bolt it on. It's a better option than outright stealing plates, which then get reported as stolen.
>
> I've purchased forged registrations and car insurance cards on the darknet. Those, along with my fake DL, will

pass first inspection by a cop, but if he/she decides to walk back to their car and run my info, I'm done for.

If that happens, then I punch it, off on another high-speed chase. In Utah I was able to buy my truck under my girlfirend's name, which eased my driving fears a bit, but when I ran from Utah to Colorado, the cops decided to classify the truck as stolen, to aid other agencies in their hunt for me.

I don't know if this technical stuff is interesting?

Completely interesting, though miserable-sounding, especially with Big Brother's march toward total domination, squeezing the traditional bank-robbing fugitive art of license-plate borrowing into historical artifact.

I asked Cousin Danny if he thought he was mentally unstable, referencing a Facebook barrage his mother, Aunt Kris, had sent when he had first been arrested all those years ago. She had just discovered social media and hammered every discovery, every lawyer note, every call to prayer into the algorithm. Bipolar disorder explained why her son had gone bad, so I asked him.

Mentally unstable?

I might be a psychopath. Or a sociopath. Or both. Check it out . . .

Cousin Danny proceeded to post a story from *Psychology Today* that detailed the difference between sociopaths and psychopaths. Sociopaths, it read, were marked by nervousness, easy agitation, and volatility. They were generally uneducated and appeared messy and generally uncool. Psychopaths, on the other hand, were clean, calm, in charge of themselves, their behaviors, and able to bend others with advanced manipulation. Wearing ties, smiling broadly, making everyone feel okay while being naughty.

> Maybe I'm a mix of sociopath and psychopath?
>> Ugh, not a great resume bullet point. I mean, normal people don't rob banks, right? The weird thing about reading about psychopathology is that it made me think of dear old dad . . .

Dear old dad? My hero Uncle Dave tied to psychopathology? Bullshit, again, Cousin Danny. I didn't need the Fifth Edition of the *Diagnostic and Statistical Manual of Mental Disorders* to tell me anything at all because I knew the truth. Coursons don't fall back on pop psychology or psychotherapy to explain greatness and are not cultlike at all. We are Christians, even if Cousin Danny thought he wasn't, and from a great evangelical Christian family.

Uncle Dave was a cinematic adventuring missionary the likes of which Harrison Ford only ever dreamed of being. Uncle Jonny a megachurch pastor of tens upon tens of thousands that grew from disenfranchised hippies perched in southern Oregon trees. Uncle Jimmy in Mexico, founding and running an orphanage for handicapped children. Cousin Mikey had not actually gone AWOL, just transitioned from Porsche to Toyota and was likely the best Toyota mechanic west of the 15 freeway. Cousin Christy was still dressing in all black, but her husband had given up on his Hollywood hopes and was now one of the most famous worship leaders in all of southern Oregon. Cousin Ellie's husband still mixed cocktails on Instagram but had a following tens upon tens of thousands strong. My brother Andy's secular rock band had toured with Dave Matthews and the Foo Fighters. My BeachGrit had grown to the number-two surf website, traffic-wise, in the whole world. And Cousin Danny was a fugitive on the lam, nearing the US record for bank robberies and probably the world record too.

Forty-some and counting, by my tabulations, though, again, obscured in the fog of bank robbers not wanting to admit to the full body of their work.

Categorizing, codifying, dismissing derelict genius because it strays into sinfulness goes against the very idea of grace, of loving God and sinning boldly, and I refused to even entertain Cousin Danny's attempt to color in those lines, quickly responding, "And OK OK OK do you really think you're a psychopath? An inability to empathize doesn't necessarily strike me as one of your 'problem areas.' Do you feel the description is fitting? Have you ever been to a psychologist/therapist?"

His response came swiftly.

> Yeah, I've never really felt that I'm a full-on psychopath
> (I do feel guilty about all I've done, and hate that I've
> caused others pain . . .) but others out there like to chalk
> up my misadventures to some sort of brain imbalance,
> and I don't want to be so blind to my own issues that I
> refuse to consider there might be something wrong. When
> I was awaiting trial for the bank robberies, my attorney
> hired a forensic psychologist to analyze me, and it was
> hilarious—he was like, "OK, I think our best shot is if we
> make you bipolar. Are you OK with that?" If it meant less

time in the slammer, for sure! So, that is the diagnosis we went with, and it did help some, I imagine, when the judge sentenced me. I did go to some therapy during my divorce, but honestly, it was such bullshit, and I'm super cynical—it was hard to buy in. I tried, I really tried, and I know it helps a ton of people, but I just laughed a lot behind the face I thought I was supposed to show.

A lot of psychology is guesswork, in my opinion, and seeing someone for an hour a week just couldn't begin to scratch the surface of what really makes somebody tick.

Psychiatrist/psychologist: "Yes, we can definitely help you, but you need to come in here every week for a few years, then maybe you might get better. The receptionist will be happy to take your insurance info . . ."

Hmmmmm

I shook my head with pursed lips as I read the words on my computer's dirty screen, having just scrolled away from a story I was working on about how the World Surf League's chief marketing officer had inserted her surfboard's fins backward. It was the eighth story I'd written on the incident so far, really driving the stake in to her professional surfing future.

"Come on, Cousin Danny . . ." beat through my head. "Work with me here. Push through this nonsense." He could do better than a passive acceptance of bipolar and insurance-based financial dismissal of psychiatry/psychology.

Love God *and* sin boldly. I hadn't given up on the former but was curious how the latter was developing, so I asked Cousin Danny how his dark education was progressing. Practice makes, if not perfect, then mildly better in every pastime I'd participated in—other than surfing, where practice only aggravates existing shortcomings.

Yes, I am trying to figure out how to be a better criminal, I suppose, but where to learn? So far, the interweb is my only instructor. Sadly, criminals don't do a lot of posting with how-tos. News reports give some hints. If I had any type of coding skills, I'd head in that direction, but I still would feel not great about ruining someone's credit and emptying their bank account.

Bank robbery is quicker, easier, simpler, and there's the slight seduction of that crime—the history, the public's disdain for big bank greediness, etc.

A big concern for me in a life of crime is working with other criminals. Back in prison, the #1 way guys were caught was via an informant. I would lose sleep over thinking about a partner getting caught and turning me in for a deal, so I prefer solo.

Some of the biggest dollar amount bank robberies are team efforts, but still . . . just too many wagging tongues for my taste.

If I can get out of a bank with only 5 to 10k, but no one else is involved, fine. I do know that what I put tellers through is not cool, at all. I read their statements when I was in prison, and I felt bad, but obviously not enough to dissuade me from doing it now.

I can't remember 95% of the tellers, but one guy sticks out in my mind. His hands were shaking like leaves when he was piling up the cash. "It's OK, relax, you're doing fine," I said.

He looked up, took a breath, and said, "OK thanks."

The women tellers seemed to be more courageous than the men. Again, I'm not proud that I robbed women.

Ugh.

Really? I mean, "pride" may be pushing it a bit far but, in reading, I felt much worse for the poor male teller, all shaky and inappropriately thankful. We live in an egalitarian democracy, anyhow, and feeling worse about robbing brave women than scared men didn't make an abundance of sense.

I didn't want to jinx him, thinking about the endgame, but we Christians—we Coursons—believe in jinxes as much as we believe in karma, which is to say we don't believe at all, so I asked about the endgame.

If I get caught it's a life sentence. Here's why: California still has the 3 strikes law. This means that if you're convicted for 3 violent felonies, you get a life sentence. Part of the deal for my 8 years was that I agreed to 2 strikes, for less years.

Robbery and home burglary, even if no one is touched or hurt, is considered violent, so I will get a 3rd strike, and do life. It is possible the feds could pick me up, and I could possibly do around 20 years there.

So yeah, I'm fucked.

An honest, sober assessment, but he wasn't going to get caught. Cousin Danny had been dancing this dance, robbing banks, gambling, visiting communes, online dating for three years after attempting an art-and-jewel heist after getting out of prison for robbing banks after going to nursing school. He knew what he was doing, and I was going to join him as soon as I could get a few more hints about where he was.

West of the Rockies?

Assumed.

College town?

Likely.

Within striking distance of an Indian casino?

Certainly.

Spokane, Washington?

Missoula, Montana?

Eugene, Oregon?

Still too many places to drive, still too many Starbucks to hawk, but I was getting close. Narrowing the field. Beginning to think like a fugitive. Beginning to look through fugitive eyes. If Cousin Danny was unable to handle a Virginia commune, though, there's no way he could take Eugene, Oregon.

Narrowing the field even more.

And I continued to look through those fugitive eyes as I headed north for the afternoon, driving the same freeways that Cousin Danny had used to disappear after robberies. Passing through Tustin before heading west toward Newport Beach.

My best friend Josh had recently purchased a sailing yacht, and we were having very much fun ripping it out to the Channel Islands and back. I thought, as we skimmed along at a good ten knots, how sailing might be good for the fugitive life, but then again, passports are still required at port, and sailing people are often too curious and chatty. Still, adding "pirate" to "bank robber," "art-and-jewel thief," and "fugitive" seemed worth the risk, and I emailed Cousin Danny the sentiment, along with a *New York Times* article called "The Secrets of the Wave Pilots" as soon as I got home after a customary sushi meal at Nobu. Looking around at the diners enjoying their yellowtail sashimi with jalapeno while mentally practicing identity theft. The wave pilots were Marshall Islanders who could navigate thousands of open ocean miles by feeling the refracting swells off islands. Absolutely ridiculous, and an ability I'd gladly rob a bank for.

> Nobu—nice! Where did you end up sailing? No worries at all about the gaps between messages—I can't imagine how crazy things are for you these days, and it's great to hear from you in spite of all that. I moved to a new place, and the Wi-Fi here is really bad, so it takes a long time to even type these messages. Give me a couple of days to get back to a coffee shop. I'll check out the NY Times magazine article, and in the meantime, I am willing to teach you how to count cards (ha!), or you could spend like ten minutes reading online how to do it. Any monkey can figure it out. It just takes practice, and even when one is skilled at it, it still only increases one's odds slightly. OK, the Wi-Fi here is super annoying right now—I'll get back with some good stuff in a day or two.

I looked forward to my card-counting lesson and planned to go try my new skill at the nearby Ocean's Eleven Casino, just off the Interstate 5. I eagerly logged on the next morning to see if he had sorted a coffee shop.

Tucson, Arizona?

And again the next morning, then periodically throughout the day, finding time to write a series of articles on Laird Hamilton's coffee creamer.

Laramie, Wyoming?

And again the next morning.

Reno, Nevada?

And again the next morning.

Albuquerque, New Mexico?

CHAPTER 20

GET DOWN. GET THE FUCK DOWN, NOW.

Cousin Danny had seen the two cop SUVs parked on the corner, exactly one block away from his small apartment, and instantly been jolted. Nerves always raw began firing that something was wrong, but he steadied himself and observed throughout the day, peeking through his curtains, not leaving, not seeing any cops.

The SUVs were still there the next day, still without cops, and he continued his vigilance, heart jumping into throat every time a car would slow over the speed bump directly in front of his door. He knew the speed bump was there, knew that cars always slowed for it, but each one sounded like the heat closing in.

On day three, the cop cars were no longer there, but now Cousin Danny was thoroughly unnerved and began looking for another place to live, finding a fully furnished basement apartment on Craigslist on the opposite side of town.

He kicked himself for not swapping the truck he had made his getaway in (after that failed Boulder bank robbery turned police chase) for another vehicle. He had new fake license plates, a new fake registration, but the FBI and all law enforcement agencies still had a description of the truck, and it was a completely unnecessary risk to continue driving it. He would find something new after he moved.

He didn't kick himself, though, for recently hopping on a Greyhound bus bound for Fort Collins, Colorado, to see his Denver girlfriend, the one whose heart he shattered with a last-minute confession before fleeing to Kansas for a shopping spree. They spent a reality-bending weekend at the local Holiday Inn, checking in as "Jack Allison and friend." That was love.

Jack Allison was his best fake name yet, or at least most literarily appealing, and he could get used to it. Was getting used to it as it was him now, to hell with Scott Hopkins, and the weekend alternated between inspired and mundane. One second his jilted lover planning to move to Florida with him and start a whole new life harboring a fugitive, the next calculating risk versus reward.

Like John Wojtowicz said, though, "Love is very strange thing. Some people feel it more deeply than others." And Cousin Danny felt it. The Florida business sounded great to him, but he also knew the fugitive life from the inside, and when the weekend ended with him running back to the Greyhound in cold sleet, a fake mustache starting to slide off his face, his Denver girlfriend watching him tearfully from her car, he thought she had made the right call.

The trip home was lonely and miserable, and he had alternated between lonely and miserable and boozy and lusty since returning, meeting a personal trainer on Tinder and using her to numb Jack Allison's pain. They would take long hikes in the surrounding woods, go on mountain-bike rides, eat at restaurants, drink at bars.

Living the life he had decided to live after turning his back on hippies and their communes. Spending bank-robbery dollars on things other than made-from-old-tires sandals and hemp pants.

And even though he still felt completely unsteady, he refused to cower, and so the day after those police SUVs disappeared, Monday, June 11, 2018, early afternoon, he called his personal trainer and invited her to a night of local author readings at a trendy indoor-outdoor bar.

She accepted, he picked her up in his truck, and as the sun slid down the sky, they drove downtown. Locals milled about in the unseasonably warm evening air. Made small talk about the just-wrapped G7 summit in Canada, where President Donald J. Trump had pushed for the re-inclusion of Russia.

Trump was all anyone talked about these days.

An obvious derangement.

Cousin Danny ordered bespoke whiskeys for him and his date. Some of her friends were there, and the group of them now joined those around in making small talk about Trump's presidency before eventually moving outside to the chairs that had been set up in a semicircle around small outdoor firepits. A stage with a microphone had been set up on the far end, where the local authors would be doing their readings.

He glanced around the crowd that was beginning to fill the remaining seats. Most were dressed casually like him and his date. Shorts and T-shirts. Many more in sport sandals. Everything fairly typical, until his eyes locked in on a square-jawed, cropped-haired face with blue eyes laser-focused on him. Those eyes darted away instantly, and Cousin Danny thought, "Cop." Then he thought, "Stop being paranoid."

The readings began, then ended without much to note. A passage on fly-fishing. One on single motherhood. How to be "awake." Mother Earth. At the end, Cousin Danny, his date, and her Tinder-adjacent friends lingered, had another drink, then said their goodnights. Square jaw, cropped hair was still there too, but again, he was bored of the three long days of intense anxiety and finally enjoying himself.

He grabbed his date's hand after the last hug, and they walked out of the bar toward his parked truck. She looked up at him, happy. He looked down at her . . .

BOOOOOOOM!

A shockwave of light and sound cut him in half. Completely blinded him and filled his ears with cotton. He froze, his date froze, for what seemed like an eternity.

Screeching tires.

A guttural scream, "DOWN! DOWN! GET THE FUCK DOWN NOW! NOW! DOWN ON THE GROUND!"

A German shepherd barking, snapping, snarling inches away from his exposed neck.

A gloved hand pressing his ear into the warm cement.

Cousin Danny was lifted up and marched to a waiting cop SUV, shoved in the back seat, and smashed his head against the metal grating separating him from the steering wheel, gas pedal, freedom.

Fuck.

Fuck. Fuck. Fuck. Fuck. Fuck.

He could feel his breath whispering those fucks but couldn't feel his bloodied head, knees, elbows, hips. Could feel that entrapment that he once knew all too well.

Fuck.

The SUV's door was pulled open violently, and a smirking FBI agent wearing that ubiquitous dark-blue FBI windbreaker was shoving a picture of his own smirking face into his own grim one. A picture taken with his Denver girlfriend's phone.

"Is this you?" the agent asked.

Cousin Danny refused to answer, staring straight ahead.

"Yeah, that's you." The agent continued, undaunted. "You know, you had quite a run there . . . you're a hard man to find." And he chuckled as he slammed the door shut.

Cousin Danny looked out the window at his personal trainer being interrogated. Imagining the horror she certainly must be feeling as she was told Jack Allison was actually Daniel David Courson. Bank robber, jewel-and-art thief, fugitive.

He smashed his head back into the metal grating, assuming he was done for. A life spent in a cage. Thinking, inexplicably, of his dad. My Uncle Dave. A man that he held in little regard, for his apparent manipulations of church congregations, a man who had destroyed his family, a man who had elevated adventure above all else except God.

Detective Ryan Newton couldn't believe that his nemesis, his Moby Dick, his Courson had done it. Couldn't believe that he had actually reached back out to the very same Denver girlfriend who had called *him* just a few short months ago. Ratting that Courson out to *him*.

He pressed her on it multiple times. "Why did he tell you who he was, that he was a bank robber, a fugitive? That his name was Daniel Courson?"

"He said he loved me . . ." was all she could offer in response, through tears.

Well, love is, in fact, a very strange thing, and some people feel it more deeply than others. Cousin Danny must have felt it deeply, which he had certainly deemed worth gambling on. Newton decided to stay on this lead, and he kept eyes on her movements. When she left, unexpectedly, for a weekend in Fort Collins, it felt hinky, so he called the FBI and sorted out a Stingray for a couple weeks' engagement outside this jilted lover's home.

Stingrays are another tool in the ever-expanding surveillance box. The ACLU describes them as "devices that mimic cell phone towers, sending out signals to trick cell phones in the area into transmitting their locations and identifying information."

Their usage against Americans is fraught with civil rights issues. They don't require obtaining a subpoena. But they are also highly effective. Every call made from her home, on her cell phone, was tracked. Every outgoing. Every incoming.

She didn't notice the dark SUV parked a block away when returning from Fort Collins. Why would she? Denver was an SUV kinda town, to begin with, and she was still busy alternately cursing herself for not moving to Florida on a whim, praising herself for not moving to Florida on a whim, cursing herself for allowing Scott . . . Dan to worm his way in once again. Cursing herself for failing to live the cinematic life that had just been offered.

He'd call, they'd talk, she'd curse herself. She'd call friends. She'd call work. She'd call restaurants, the gas company, the cable company, then he'd call again, and records of each of them began piling up. Not actual transcripts, but numbers and one, in particular, emanating from Boise, Idaho.

The interdepartmental coordination took a few days. Boise Police Department planted two SUVs near the cell tower that the vast majority of those calls were pinging off of. When they were reasonably sure they had a match, they coordinated between the local FBI branch, SWAT team, and detectives, observing their suspect's home, running the information on the Toyota parked out front, gathering every advantage they possibly could.

Then, one unseasonably warm spring night, he stepped out, walked to his truck, drove to an unidentified woman's home, picked her up, then drove downtown, posting up in a trendy indoor-outdoor bar that featured firepits. Three plainclothes detectives tried to mingle, casually, while guarding the exits and keeping eyes on him. They didn't want to take him here—too many people—and while Daniel David Courson had not displayed a tendency for wanton violence, there is no telling what a trapped man might do in a moment of sheer panic.

Thankfully he lingered after the series of local author readings wrapped, even ordering another drink. And he seemed completely oblivious, casual even, grabbing his date's hand and pressing out to the street.

The plan was executed perfectly. A flashbang grenade shot across his path. SWAT vehicles, PD SUVs, and FBI sedans screeching around the corner. The K9 team keeping him down while they searched for weapons, cuffed, and stuffed him.

Detective Newton received the call ten minutes after it was confirmed that they had their man. He was still at his desk. He thanked the team then thrust his hands triumphantly in the air, laughing at the photo his partner had tacked to the wall. Cousin Danny's smiling mug with the words "You'll find Courson someday . . . psych!" scrawled underneath.

CHAPTER 21

WRITER'S RETREAT

On the fifth morning without an encrypted email, not bothering with darknet search engines, I decided to Google "Daniel Courson" just for kicks, just to revel in his past greatness, and was punched in the face by six simple words.

"FBI suspect arrested in downtown Boise."

There's no way this was Cousin Danny.

I clicked.

And read about Boise Police, working with the FBI, arresting a fugitive named Daniel David Courson who was wanted for bank robbery, fleeing California, driving a stolen Toyota Tacoma.

Son of a bitch.

I knew it was in the cards, already thought it had happened, in fact. He knew it was in the cards, though didn't act like it, but here it officially was. The end of the line.

Boise, Idaho.

How had I missed Boise, Idaho?

Of course it was Boise, Idaho. I could have been there, should have been there, close enough to Ernest Hemingway's final resting place. America's greatest writer, like Cousin Danny, had been paranoid about the FBI in his last days, worrying that they had a file on him and were tracking his movements. They were, indubitably. J. Edgar Hoover had expanded his power from those early Dillinger days and was busy keeping tabs on every American deemed "irregular," though he didn't have the power of a Stingray at his disposal, and Papa didn't have a cell phone.

Boise, Idaho.

I should have been there, staking out middle-class white social hotspots that hosted local author readings. I should have been driving the US-20 back and forth between Ketchum and Boise with eyes peeled for Cousin Danny, with a quick swing of illegal trespass into the house where Ernest Hemingway loosed a shotgun into his head.

I could have found him if I had really tried, and been with him on the lam and witnessed how it really truly looked—and maybe even helped him rob a bank because my wife took part in an act of social disobedience against the Trump presidency. Like, *really* socially disobedient and having to flee the country with cash on hand FAST.

An adventurous chimera, because my heart only beat in those adventurous rhythms, but now it was over. Cousin Danny was off the lam. He was back in the claw, the jaws, of a system. Of *the* system.

I slumped in my chair, depressed.

I knew he would get caught, eventually. Like missing being an astronaut and shooting for doctor then missing doctor and becoming a nurse, Cousin Danny's path had not been one of unmitigated success. It was part of why Nana had loved him so much—the gangly snake-bit parts of his life, his light failures, all the way down to bank-robber fugitive. He wasn't "charmed." He overvalued his craftiness and undervalued the craftiness of those chasing him. He pushed for exotic adventure yet couldn't shake online dating.

It was only a matter of time until his stumble, and his stumble had come. Just like when he'd left half a fingerprint on a ripped piece of latex glove at a bank in California. Just like when he had made his prison break while two ex–San Diego State University track star EMTs were working. Just like when he decided to lift art and jewels when their owner was coming home.

I had no idea how to reach Cousin Danny, to know which prison he was in or what his near-future held, just imagined him sitting in a holding cell somewhere looking at what had to be a life sentence.

Robbing banks, getting out, heisting art and jewels, running from the law while robbing more banks. How could it not be a life sentence? And he would soon have his own set of vacuous eyes that he had witnessed on others serving life sentences during his first eight-year prison stretch.

I had tried to set him up for the upside of that possibility, at least literarily. I told him to write, that first prison stretch, and continued to push while he was on the lam, half-joking that he'd be exceedingly lucky when he finally got caught. Telling him that endless time to sit and write would be so glorious. With a life sentence, every written sentence could be made perfect and woven seamlessly into every other perfect-written sentence, eventually forming the great American novel and shaming David Foster Wallace in the process. Maybe even Ernest Hemingway himself. He would be on a perpetual writer's retreat. A writer's retreat without end.

Amen.

CHAPTER 22

YOU'VE NEVER BEEN TO HEAVEN, BUT YOU GOT PRETTY CLOSE LAST NIGHT

So there I was, again, in the front yard attempting to clean up thousands of tiny pieces of hundreds of water balloons from my daughter's most recent all-out war with her best friend, a Japanese girl with a penchant for punk rock disruption lost on our lame modern world, when the mail jalopy came rumbling to a stop in front of the driveway. The postman, still a bro, seemed like he wasn't in a hurry while handing me an array of mail.

"Surf looked lousy today."

"I think it was."

"Water balloons?"

"Yeah."

"Cool."

He drove off without a shaka but still leaving a puff of diesel smoke as a lingering memory.

Dang kid and her water-balloon offensives. A rainbow of disaster everywhere. Not chill but decidedly punk. I left it behind, flipping through the small stack. A plea to renew the Legoland California annual pass, an American Girl doll catalog, an overdue dermatology bill, a letter from Federal Correctional Victorville, Medium 1. I paused with happy anticipation.

Bingo.

Cousin Danny had done it, really done it. He had turned his lockup into a writer's retreat, and the chapters were coming once, sometimes twice, a week. I wandered over to the patio, letting that rainbow disaster lie in state, thinking about making my daughter clean it up instead, though I knew that would never work.

I pulled out a black chair and sat down knowing exactly what Victorville, California, feels like in late Autumn. My other daughter is a world-class soccer player, and I'd spent months watching her play various tournaments in Victorville. Apparently, jails and world-class soccer facilities covet the same hideous stretches of godforsaken, windblown, hot-unless-they're-freezing, dry, population-center-adjacent stretches of earth.

Victorville feels like hell.

I studied the envelope, like I did each time one of his letters, his chapters, arrived. Imagining the journey that it had been through, from prison cell through censors to mail bro then me on my patio.

Thrilled.

Its flap peeled open as easily as each before it, and I dug in with fancy Montblanc editing pen already in my pocket, though I didn't really need it anymore. I was along for the damned ride.

CHAPTER 11

Few experiences are more demeaning than a prison transfer. Processed. Numbered. Lined up, loaded and unloaded like pressed ham. I kneeled as my ankle shackles and leg chains were clicked on, along with a chain around my waist, handcuffs, fully trussed up and ready for a new temporary home. I drearily, slowly climbed into the steel cage that was set into the rear of a nondescript passenger van and asked the officer driving where we were going.

"Geo. Private prison." He told me.

I wondered if the billionaire shareholders of places like Geo had possibly reinvested some of their profits to make the joint more habitable than the Hole. Maybe my situation was looking up. If I was being sent away, brushed under the rug after I refused to plead guilty to the bullshit charge of assaulting an officer, I hoped that at least my confinement conditions might improve for my trouble. An hour later, after my neck got sore from gawking at the real world again through the iron-grated windows, we arrived.

The first thing I saw as we rolled up to the GEO/ICE Processing Center in Aurora, Colorado, was protestors, lots of them, and they were mad. They were mad. They were mostly family members of inmates, locked up not for criminal behavior, but for being in the US illegally, now awaiting deportation to countries all over the world.

The US Marshals rented one of the dozens of housing modules in the facility for overflow federal inmates, or "problem" prisoners like me. I do meet dudes with fascinating stories in here—case in point: "The Cannibal," my coworker. Yup, he killed and consumed his wife. Not sure if Chianti and fava beans were involved. He's creepy.

Uncle Dave had always had a thing for cannibals too, visiting those ones in Papua New Guinea's highlands when I was six, gifting them some dental care, and also building his cinder block mausoleum in Vanuatu, which has a famous cannibal tradition.

Cousin Danny had been shuttled to jails in Colorado and Nevada, rubbing elbows with prison celebrities along the way, though he had been in California for a year, the most notable inmate in Victorville's long history, besides Philadelphia Phillies all-star Lenny Dykstra.

Staring down a forty-year sentence, Cousin Danny managed to get called "bitch" by a guard, demand a retraction (since "bitch" is the biggest insult behind bars), then got smashed by that guard and all his friends, leading to a trip in the Hole and all the disciplinary proceedings that accompanied.

The last time Cousin Danny had been called a bitch, behind bars, was during his first stretch, by a cellmate who had portraits of Hitler, Mussolini, and Himmler tattooed on his back with "Deutschland über Alles" on both shoulders—complete with umlaut. Ira would spend the majority of each day pacing their shared space repeating single German words over and over, trying to learn his heart's language.

One day, Ira called Cousin Danny a bitch for dropping a ramen noodle onto his bunk. Ira was notoriously violent, and Cousin Danny didn't want to have to fight him, because Coursons aren't, historically, trained fighters. But to let a "bitch" slide would have guaranteed perpetual abuse, so Cousin Danny waited until Ira turned his head slightly, then tried to kick it, grazing his nose.

Ramen be damned, Ira jumped off his bunk, and the two stood face to face for an eternal moment before smashing each other's jaws. Ira made the next move, pulling Cousin Danny close and biting his nose. Cousin Danny saw the blood and thought his nose might have been bitten off. Staring that noseless future in the face, he stepped back slightly then sent his forehead into Ira's nose once, twice, three times, forcing him to stumble back. Cousin Danny felt his face, nose still there though wet—a relief. But now he was filled with rage, and while Coursons, historically, aren't trained fighters, we fill with rage like no other.

Once, while driving from Cardiff-by-the-Sea to Santa Barbara for a weekend of glamping in a refurbished zoo with friends, we all became hungry and decided that sushi would be just the thing. There's a Sugarfish in Calabasas, the Kardashians' ancestral home, and the crew was all very excited, swinging in, getting a table, trying to order off-menu for the children as they only like avocado maki rolls.

Sugarfish doesn't have avocado maki rolls, though, and doesn't allow for off-menu ordering. The founder, sushi master Kazunori Nozawa, makes zero exceptions, and the mealy mouthed waiter told me as much.

"Fine," I responded, as there was a Vons grocery store in the same fancy strip mall—Calabasas is composed entirely of fancy strip malls—and I left as soon as he took our generous order to go fetch the kids their avocado maki rolls.

I returned, fifteen minutes later, cracked open the Vons sushi, and tucked into my Kirin Ichiban while sampling the first round of sushi that had already been delivered to the table. Before I enjoyed my second morsel, though, our waiter was breathing down my neck.

"Excuse me, sir. We don't allow outside food in the restaurant."

"Are you kidding me?" I responded. "This is a strip mall."

"Sir." He said unbending. "We can't allow that."

Rage just starting to bubble, I told him to send the manager out and I would deal with him and him exclusively. The manager came out and repeated the same waiter talk. I told him they didn't have avocado maki rolls on the menu, wouldn't accommodate, and I simply solved the problem. Win-win. He maintained his ground: they did not allow outside food in the restaurant, and my rage went from bubble to geyser.

"YOU DON'T? IN A STRIP MALL? FUCK YOU!"

And now my wife was caught up in the action, a famous ex-professional snowboarder-cum-sports agent but Hessian underneath it all and always itching for a fight. She jumped to her feet, motioning to the table filled with sushi with much more on the way, declaring how much money we were spending, how much more we were about to spend.

The manager was unbending, and so I almost flipped the table over while we pulled our kids and friends up by the collars and forced them to storm out, with the rest of the diners having stopped their eating and staring at this unnecessary scene, including *Beverly Hills 90210*'s Brian Austin Green, his then-wife actress Megan Fox (pre–Machine Gun Kelly), and their children.

A deluge of rage completely out of order, in retrospect, but a deluge nonetheless.

Cousin Danny had beaten that former neo-Nazi cellmate into submission, tapping into that Courson rage and refusing to buckle. On this latest insult, he insisted that he was in the right and the guard was out of line, so he got shipped to yet another Colorado prison, the for-profit one where Detective Newton came to see him face to face, acting like a fan more than a cop plying for information.

And as a bonus for misbehavior, in Colorado, Cousin Danny got stuck with a methamphetamine dealer who spoke, in great detail, about all the children he was going to molest when he got out, plus all the stockpiles of weapons he had stashed all over the greater western United States for the war he was going to wage against the entire United States and its cursed justice system.

Or something.

Cousin Danny had never wanted to be a prison rat, loathed the very idea like he loathed the guards, but children are children, and so he coughed up the details, which turned out to be both serious enough and verifiable enough to get himself shipped to Victorville, then maybe Oregon or Utah with thirty-plus years lopped off his sentence.

Highly intelligent. He'll be out plenty young enough to leave Carl Gugasian in the dust, if he so chooses. And I'm thinking about the ethics of encouraging this bold sin, this pushing the US record for bank robberies and probably the world record too. Really pondering if it was okay to continue pushing the bolder sin without yet really trying to rehabilitate the love of God.

When he had been on the lam, and right when I was thickly wondering about the Courson disinterest in our captive, he wrote:

> I told you nobody wrote or visited me while I was locked
> up that first time, but that wasn't accurate. Three Coursons
> wrote to me regularly, which was kind. My dad wrote to
> me almost daily. It's nice to hear your name called at mail

call, but his cards and letters were all the same. "We're praying for you, dear, dear son, and so proud of you."

Really?

Nana wrote a lot too, which was kind of her, and I know she was physically going downhill, and she meant well.

The funniest letters were from Ben Courson. I'm no writer (obviously), but his letters seemed to be penned by a fifth grader, writing to his parents from summer camp. It was super weird—they were overly optimistic, reassuring me that Jesus would help me, and that I was so inspiring to everyone.

Again, really?

I wish I could say that I wrote back how I really felt, but I just leaned toward placating them, and told them what they wanted to hear, that yes, Jesus was in fact taking time out of his busy schedule and helping me so, so much. I knew that's what they wanted to hear, so I just did it.

Kind of a dick move.

And I was thinking about this, again, reading about his handcuffs and shackles, the Hole and for-profit prisons in the United States, where billons are made off Cousin Danny's back, and thousands upon thousands more captives that Jesus came to set free when the brown wooden gate in front of my house slides open and Cousin Benny stands before me, tall and handsome and electric.

Ben is an even better dictionary definition of West Coast WASP than I am. Tall, thin, blue-eyed, almost-brown hair that turns blond with enough skateboarding, an Anglo-Saxon combination that is neither fancy nor interesting, just white.

The luck. Or rather predestination.

"Benny!" I greeted him loudly while setting Cousin Danny's Chapter 11 down.

"Hey, Chas . . . Charlie . . . Chas!" he responds.

The Coursons have been confused as to what name to call me since I became a surf journalist, as I had always been Cousin Charlie to them. I don't exactly know why I started using "Chas" when I wrote. It was something my father regularly called me, but, more importantly in retrospect, it sounded like an asshole name. A person that fathers and mothers eventually disown.

"What are you doing in Cardiff-by-the-Sea?" I continued, not caring what he called me unless he called me "Chuck." Anyone who ever calls me "Chuck" hates me, even though being "Chuck Smith" is exactly where I belong, and in the end, is where I might mercifully end up.

"I had a speaking thing at a church in Orange County, another one down here, then I'm flying out later tonight. How are you doing, cousin? Have you been to any cool countries lately? What are you reading? Hey . . . we have to go skateboard in North Korea together."

Cousin Benny had taken up skateboarding recently, and just taken over Uncle Jonny's megachurch as head pastor. Uncle Jonny's youngest son had been on a rocket to evangelical fame since his early Sunday School days, growing up with as much charisma as the great big tent revival preachers of Nana's youth. As handsome as Billy Graham. As well-spoken. Even as a preteen, he combined a relentless enthusiasm for the gospel with an ability to deliver it in rapid-fire staccato pops. Child pastors, teachers, inspirationalists were nothing new in Christianity. Jesus had reprimanded his disciples for keeping young ones away from him in Matthew 19:14, "Suffer little children, and forbid them not, to come unto me: for of such is the kingdom of heaven." Children had been martyred for their belief at the beginnings of the church, led crusades in the Middle Ages, had faith healed in the renaissance, and packed meeting fields in the industrial days, calling on sinners to repent, for their kingdom of heaven was at hand. Heck, Uncle Jonny had gotten his preaching start at sixteen.

Cousin Benny had flair, even as a tween, and while his unbridled eagerness may have rubbed Cousin Danny the wrong way while he was in the midst of captivity, at least Cousin Benny wrote. At least he was curious about the wayward Courson and did the evangelical thing by "encouraging the captive."

And while I could understand Cousin Danny's relative annoyance, I couldn't help but be impressed with Cousin Benny's skill. With his taking the Courson mantle on properly. He is good. He is effective. He is the future. And he had just published his third smash bestselling book, this one titled *Flirting with Darkness* and detailing his own struggle with depression and suicidal thoughts and the Biblical response. Christian publishing being the last bastion of hope in the book world. Randall Cunningham, one of the greatest quarterbacks of all time, godfather of the run-and-gun offenses that gave birth to the varietal of football we so enjoy today, called Cousin Benny's book "a playbook that will equip downcast souls to play offense and defeat depression!"

Cousin Benny asked me for a blurb too, and I should have attempted to approach Randall Cunningham's poetry, but I crassly wrote, "Rejoice always. We live in a damned fallen world. A troubled world. An impossible-to-sort, mind-bending, impossibly sad world, but there is still joy. There is always joy. Ben Courson may be young, but son of a bitch if he don't write a way forward. A way through the darkness. Rejoice, always." Which got whittled down to "'A way forward through darkness'—Chas Smith, journalist for *Surfing Magazine*" by the book's publisher. *Surfing Magazine* had been completely defunct for five years prior to *Flirting with Darkness*'s publication.

But North Korea?

"Wait, North Korea? Why do you want to go to North Korea?"

"I was reading your book about surfing with al-Qaeda, and we have to. Fire! How?"

"I don't think you really want to go to North Korea. Yemen after 9/11 was a misunderstood, wild Middle East. Sure, it was considered rogue, I guess, but there was still freedom of discovery. Hard to access but available. Dirty and raw, but dirty and raw. I think when you go to North Korea, you just become a pawn of their heavy state-sponsored propaganda."

"We still have to. Have you ever trained with a Navy SEAL? I want to get working on my fantasy trilogy, but my publisher only wants me to do Christian self-help books. I have the first two mostly written and the third one all mapped out. I wrote them all on my phone. That has to count for something. What are you reading?" he asked again, eyeing Cousin Danny's prison letter.

"A letter from our Cousin Danny. Did you ever go visit him?"

"No, but I wrote him. Is he still in prison? What did you think of Camus's opinions on human struggle?"

"He's actually back in prison after getting out, failing at a jewel-and-art heist, heading out on the lam, robbing more banks, and getting caught again, but he's sniffing the all-time record for bank robberies by my calculations. And I love everything Camus ever did but also think he should have rounded the bend and converted to Catholicism."

This string of ridiculous stopped Cousin Benny in his verbal tracks.

"Whoa. What?"

I walked him through the last decade, how Cousin Danny had moved back to North County, San Diego, upon his release from Richard J. Donovan's Correctional Facility, then how he had really gone all in, eluding the FBI for years before being undone by Tinder in Idaho. There was a short pause before Cousin Benny unexpectedly began hammering the police.

"Oh man, I really hate cops. I get pulled over all the time in Medford, and it's all I can do not to freak out and scream. I almost got arrested skateboarding in Italy. Power-tripping for no reason, and what do you think of Black Lives Matter? I know there is controversy about the Marxism or whatever, but I don't care and preached BLM from the pulpit the other night because it's about the broad strokes here, and the message is important. Christians need to be uncomfortable."

Whoa. What?

Severely disliking law enforcement and preaching Black Lives Matter from the pulpit in southern Oregon? Cousin Danny and Cousin Benny are a lot closer than either realized, and closer to me too, all closer to Uncle Dave—and this Courson DNA more volatile than Nana ever dreamed.

Family. Fame. Secrets. Cinder block mausoleums. Scared and scarred bank tellers. Dreams of North Korea. But above all, the ridiculous grace of God even when it's not wanted.

I thought about calling Uncle Jonny with Cousin Benny right there and peppering him with quality surf-journalist questions, getting to the bottom of it all, but I knew Uncle Jonny would only laugh in his slow, measured way and say something like, "You know Charlie—Chas—Charlie, the Lord has always chosen unlikely champions. Noah got drunk and fell asleep naked in his tent. Abraham disobeyed God and went to Egypt instead of staying in the land promised him. David, the man after God's own heart, stole the general of his army's wife, then sent him off the front lines to kill him. Peter, on whom Jesus declared the church would be built, denied Jesus three times before he was crucified. Paul hunted Christians and sent them to their deaths before converting himself. It's all a fucking shit show. God loves the mess." He wouldn't have actually said the last part, but it's true.

God, historically, loves a mess.

Uncle Jonny had also severely mellowed his own politics over the years, Republicanism no longer an important part of the DNA. Conservatism all but vanished. He preached more and more rarely, but when he did he focused on love, acceptance, and forgiveness, his latest sermon delivered in his now iconic cadence, flavored with a warmth only deep, profound, and abiding faithfulness can bring.

"As you get older you really do realize what does matter and what doesn't matter, and theological arguments, or doctrinal divisions, or political perspectives, and—you know, it's a curious thing," Uncle Jonny said, sitting back on his stool, eyes crinkling, mouth smiling. "At the end of the day, you realize none of that matters. Not really. If I have the tongues of men and angels, and if I have all knowledge and understand all mysteries, and even if I give my body to be burning out in ministry, and if I give all my goods to feed the poor but I have not love, I am nothing."

Mess and love. Love and mess.

The gospel, in short.

"What did Cousin Danny do again, when he got out of prison?" Cousin Benny cut into my mental Uncle Jonny pondering. "Tried to steal jewels and art then started robbing banks again while on Tinder dates? And what is he going to do when he gets out again?"

"Exactly." I responded. "Or not exactly, but close, and I don't know the exact number, but he's sniffing the US record for bank robberies and probably the world record too. How can we not encourage him to go for it? I know, decidedly not Christian, and maybe illegal to even suggest, but we're Coursons, or you two are. We climb K2, we smuggle Stinger missiles into Afghanistan, we—"

"—skate North Korea!" Cousin Benny thrusted a fist in the air, cutting me off.

"Have you ever heard of Otto Warmbier?" I asked, but then checked myself and my lame non-bank-robbing, non-fugitive-living pulled punch. "Sure. We're gonna skate North Korea, but, uh . . ." And I imagined how horrible this was all going to be, considering North Korea and its inherent adventure flaws but also the fact that Cousin Benny doesn't really ride a skateboard. He rides some aberrant soft-wheeled longboard monstrosity. But what the world requires of the Coursons is that they continue to be Coursons and, as a Smith, I'd better go too.

POSTSCRIPT

Except North Korea was not to be.

A few short months after Cousin Benny bounced like Tigger out of my brown wooden gate onto yet another speaking engagement, another packed sanctuary, another wildly successful book signing, carrying the future on his broad shoulders, Nana's evangelical Camelot came crashing down in a heap.

Summer had turned to fall, the cleaning of water balloons in the yard replaced by the nibbling of appetizers and drinking of drinks at Applebee's in Kearny Mesa, around the literal corner from Cousin Danny's first bank hit. My daughter had both discovered and been discovered by ballet and spent hours a day inside a dull, flat, one-story building that housed a world-class academy. Rond de jambe-ing, tendu-ing, pirouette-ing.

While she strove for artistic greatness, with a statuesque instructor barking at her to "be allergic to average," I sat munching chips, drinking Grey Goose and sodas, alternating between picking on Kelly Slater and applying the end to the very book you are now finishing. Dreaming about the glory of my first bank being Cousin Danny's first bank but still not being able to craft the right narrative that would necessitate me robbing it; of my daughter getting cast in Moscow's Bolshoi, London's Royal, Paris's Opéra and needing . . .

Argh.

She won't need any of my nonsense, dang little overachiever. She'll be able to charm Moscow, London, Paris with her own long neck, longer legs, and average allergy.

I had just gotten a long letter from Cousin Danny, anyhow, a sort of bank robbery for dummies, detailing the real basics, and it was wonderful. "There are many different ways to make money that run afoul of the law," it began, before cascading magnificently:

> One of the simplest, dumbest, quickest is bank robbery. Any monkey can do it, but the problem is the reward-to-risk ratio: The payoff is relatively low, and the consequences of getting caught are severe. In the eyes of the courts, no matter the method, even the timid note-passers, it's all considered a violent felony, and that equals anywhere from 5 to 20 years in the slammer . . . not some low-level Club Fed prison camp, either. It's off to a fuck-you-in-the-ass/ join-a-prison-gang/carry-a-shank-at-all-times gladiator-dome–type of place.
>
> If making a buck illegally is an actual reality, it's much better to invest a little time educating yourself about identity theft, embezzlement, securities fraud, or credit-card cloning. Much higher yields than a quick robbery, and way less prison time to be spent at a low-level prison camp with Martha Stewart crochet classes and weekend BBQs with the fam, if caught.

Yes, bank robbery does have its draws. There's the obvious street cred that comes with a timeless classic of antisocial behavior; rushing into a bank and relieving it of its cash à la John Dillinger. It's a perfect prescription for those of us suffering from addiction to instant gratification . . . two minutes of effort, stacks of Benjamins, get away, and done. Short attention span crime, no muss, no fuss.

There's not even a need to get rough—in none of my robberies did I even touch another human or point a gun. Violence is completely unnecessary and, frankly, just poor form. The tellers are trained to give a thief whatever they ask for, quickly, compliantly, with zero confrontation. Insurance bean-counters long ago computed that it's much cheaper to hand over some cash than pay out or settle a lawsuit by a teller who was instructed to resist then shot.

Also, all the money in a robbery is reimbursed via insurance and the federal government, so while technically not a victimless crime, it's damn close. Another tick in the pro column.

And it's just so easy to do, no harder than being an asshole at the Olive Garden and demanding to see the manager because there's a pube in my fettucine Alfredo. The feeble defensive measures employed by banks are there more for the comfort of customers than actual robbery prevention. It's no wonder dozens of bank robberies are pulled every week in the US, mostly going unsolved.

There is a jump from the one- or two-time bank robbers to that next echelon, the serial bank robber. Once the basics of hitting a bank are grasped, it becomes a rinse-and-repeat process. Like an assembly line worker. I barely remember going through the motions, and living on the run became my mundane reality. Planning the next bank robbery, coffee and laptop before me, turned into a routine, a job, and I learned a few things along the way.

So here's the first PowerPoint presentation on . . .

HOW TO MAKE A LIVING AS A SERIAL BANK ROBBER.

1. Embrace your newfound dark side.

   You must commit to being a fulltime criminal wholly apart from the hard-working, God-fearing good people of the world. Think of yourself as an expert liar:

   a. Develop a vague description of what you do for a living, if anyone asks. I fancied myself a "medical writer," a nebulous, vague career that would explain my long mornings at random coffee shops using varied IP addresses and VPNs to research my next bank.

   b. Learn to sprinkle in some truth with the lies. My past medical career allowed me to "talk the talk."

2. Flush away your guilt for frightening tellers and not contacting your family with personally preferred distractions.

   a. Single malt whiskey.

   b. Drugs from the darknet.

   c. Random casual sex.

   d. Therapy.

I found an excellent therapist in Park City, $100 cash per session, who I could unload my guilt on, robberies and all. Lots of tears, deep breaths, confessions, and best of all doctor-patient privilege.

3. Never lay down deep roots. Like De Niro in *Heat*, the moment you feel law enforcement closing in, turn your back on anyone and anything you've grown close to and get away.

    a. Prepare a well-stocked "go bag." A new identity, cash, clothing, disguise.

    b. Be willing to ghost a girlfriend (this was my ultimate downfall . . .)

    c. Have the next destination city and escape route planned.

4. Live within your means. You are middle-class, not some kingpin baller. Spend accordingly.

    a. Average bank take: $10,000; so at one a month: $120,000 a year.

    b. Budget your earnings like everyone else.

    c. When laundering cash through casinos, don't drown in degenerative, compulsive gambling.

5. Put in the work to plan. You've already made an idiotic decision to be a professional bank robber. The least you can do now is to do it right.

    a. Take some time to research banks using Google Maps, calculating time and distance to cop shops along with multiple getaway routes.

    b. Be sure there's no bank guard, bandit barrier, or bulletproof teller glass.

    c. Plan the best getaway method.

       i.   Sprint to car.

      ii.   Bike to car.

    iii.   Car to different car.

   d.   Decide if you prefer handing over a note or just a lot of yelling. Ask yourself, "Am I an introvert or an extrovert?"

   e.   Never rob a bank near your home.

   f.   Scan news websites after the robbery to see what evidence the cops have on you.

   g.   Review your disguise, because there will be lots of photos of you. Look your best.

   h.   Put in time searching the darknet, looking for better false identity documents and ways into and out of the country.

6.   Follow the example of those who have gone before. There are randos who rob a bank then there are bank robbers.

   a.   The internet is chock-full of the many stories and videos of bumbling oafs making every mistake in the book.

   b.   On the other end, there are the legends. People like the Friday Night Bandit, who amassed millions over several years of bank heists by adhering to a super-strict program of disciplined planning and execution.

7.   Don't believe the hype. Take the media coverage with a grain of salt.

   a.   Once you've been categorized as a serial bank robber, your case gets kicked up to the FBI. They spend many hours looking for you, and

they are smart, driven, and possess many
toys to track you down. One mistake and
they'll find you like they found me.

b. Get over your smug, self-congratulatory
superiority when you watch the TV news
reports and web pages about your little heist.
Carefully note what information the cops may
have from forensics, witnesses, etc.

8. The X-factor is real. Do enough robberies and Murphy
will show up.

a. Eventually something will not go as planned.

b. Dyed money can be cleaned with brake
cleaner and industrial detergent. I once had
dozens of C-notes hanging all over my rented
room, drying out after a dye-cleaning session.
I had to shoulder my door closed when a
housemate almost walked in, claiming I was
sick and didn't want to expose him.

c. GPS Transponders. A heroic teller may slide
one of these to you in your stacks. Telling
them not to will usually work, but when it
doesn't you must find it and chuck it quickly
or else ready yourself for a high-speed chase.
Some swear by dunking the cash in a tank
of water.

d. The valiant bystander. A worst-case scenario,
day ruiner. Risk can be mitigated by going
in when the customer count is low or zero,
but even so, a hero could walk in possibly
armed or off-duty and tackle, shoot, wrestle

you, ruining a perfectly good bank robbery.
Be aware.

9. Take the time to craft a good disguise. I applaud
   creativity. Have some fun with it.

   a. Cold weather coverup: A big snowstorm
      brings opportunity to conceal everything.

   b. Halloween costume: Darth Vader is a popular
      option with endless possibilities.

   c. COVID masking: Self-explanatory.

   d. Just be sure to completely cover up. I was
      identified by what an investigator described
      as a "distinctive nose," the only part of my
      anatomy that showed through my disguise.

10. Donate 10 percent of your take to a good cause. This is
    a great way to deal with guilt.

    a. An anonymous cash donation to a family
       member in need.

    b. A woke payment to BLM, AOC, or Antifa.

    c. A college scholarship fund to a bank teller
       putting herself/himself through school.

    d. I had my own cause that shall remain
       anonymous.

11. Never get in contact with family, friends, or lovers.

    a. This is the number one way to get caught.
       Many a fugitive has fallen prey to the pull of
       human connection. I know I did.

    b. Embrace the loner lifestyle and don't fall
       in love.

This concludes this PowerPoint presentation. As you
can see, bank robbery, along with living on the lam, is a

fool's errand. It's a crime of desperation followed by the inevitable capture, conviction, and imprisonment. Into a human warehouse of concrete cocoons that will, somehow, be miserable enough to deter any future forays to the dark side.

Maybe this second attempt at rehabilitation will finally crush my craving to buck expectations in spectacular fashion.

Maybe not.

The simplicity reminded me of Jesus's Sermon on the Mount, where our Lord laid out, in counterintuitive clarity, what it means to be a Christian. "Blessed are the poor in spirit.... Blessed are those who mourn.... Blessed are the meek...." Definitely not blessed are the bank robbers, as "Thou shalt not steal" was very clearly one of the Ten Commandments ... but also counterintuitive? How to carry it all off? I was entertaining the sacrilegious comparison between the two, trying to will one into the other, when my phone, sitting on the soapstone counter, buzzed.

A message from my sister, always true, always only integral.

"Did Mom tell you about Ben's sexual misconduct, or did you already know?"

I sat there, puzzling over what she possibly could be referring to, when the next message came through seconds later, answering any question. It was a story from "a Christian media outlet, reporting the unvarnished truth about what's happening in the Christian community," titled "Oregon Megachurch Pastor Steps Down Amid Sexual Misconduct."

Oh man, and oh no. I gingerly dropped my head, left a chip lonely in white queso dip, clicked, and read.

It was a nasty yet all-too-familiar story of excess, of power abuse, of tawdry, unfortunate ugliness. Cousin Benny had been accused of violating basic trust only shades different than any of the fallen megastar evangelists had done before him. Police reports filed; victims coming forward with embarrassing detail of compromising positions; twisted theological interpretations of "sin"; shame, deep shame.

A second story followed closely on the heels of the first, implicating Uncle Jonny in his own decades-old impropriety, plus aggrieved underlings, detailing how toiling under his leadership, over all those years, had been torturous. How they were over-worked, underpaid, broken, then dismissed without recognition.

Oh man, oh no, and proper trouble.

As the days passed, the stories continued to populate, with a Facebook group called Applegate Christian Survivors popping up and pastors taking to Instagram, demanding accountability, insisting that Cousin Benny take a lie detector test and excoriating him for turning one down, because he was clearly afraid of the nastiest of truths and of falling far, far short.

My sister and I talked regularly. She was angry that it had all devolved into this, frustrated by both the lack of imagination and the lack of accountability.

For his part, Cousin Benny disappeared entirely. His rocket to evangelical fame mothballed. Applegate scrubbed him from the church website, and while his once-robust social media account remained alive, though inactive, he himself was nowhere to be found. Not a peep, not a trace. I tried to contact him, but apparently, his phone had been thrown away. Apparently, he had taken a job pounding nails somewhere in southern Oregon. Maybe stitching handbags in Southern California.

Uncle Jonny was quickly scrubbed from Applegate's website too, though he, for his part, embarked upon a series of short YouTube vignettes, never mentioning the scandals but, instead, leaning further into his "love, acceptance, forgiveness" routine. Gently chastising those who would "judge others," calling them "grumpy bears" as opposed to "care bears"—and, of course, God doesn't want "grumpy bears," nor can he use them.

Both responses—all too common in the evangelical church—irritated me: either disappear, lick wounds, hopefully return "humbled" and triumphant, or transform God's Word into self-serving mush. The Coursons were supposed to be great—great enough to avoid clichéd traps but, if slipped into one, great enough to face the horror square and speak to it, to own it.

The fame I so admired as a child, and a Calvary Chapel evangelical model built upon famous pastors as the ideal, appeared to only lead straight into a mess. An absolute mess. Aimee Semple McPherson, Billy Sunday, Billy Graham, and others, with their indelible marks on history: What to do with them? They were flawed, misguided, mixing with the wrong crowd like early drug dealers, Richard Milhous Nixon, sinners; famous, but they were never boring. Never clichéd. Cousin Benny and Uncle Jonny, though, had instantly become dull hacks with uninventive sexual improprieties, hollow disappearings, and/or Scriptural pivotings. It made me sad, deeply sad. Nana's dream smoldering in that heap. But what to do?

When I was growing up, my father, who Nana liked even less than me, was perpetually head of local Young Life chapters. Young Life is a Presbyterian high school initiative with the mission of "introducing adolescents to Jesus Christ and helping them grow in their faith." Presbyterians were not flashy or new; simply a crusty Protestant strain founded out of the Church of Scotland in the Calvinist tradition. My father would lead weekly Young Life meetings featuring music, funny skits, games, and inspirational messages. Marshfield High School students would flock to and pack the old Carnegie Library that he and my mother had purchased, theming it "surf."

"It's a sin to bore a kid," was my father's operating principle, and as I became shattered by Cousin Benny and Uncle Jonny's disastrous boredom, I remembered what he had actually done and how he had never turned from the path. Even though I had frustrated him and my mother with empty surf journalism, even though I now regularly frequented Applebee's, I remembered the simple truth:

Boredom is a sin.

Cousin Danny had never bored, and while I may never stumble upon an actual reason to rob a bank, may never be forced into the beautiful desperation, maybe it's time for Cousin Benny to sort that out. To take Cousin Danny's mantle and Tigger-bounce to glory, for, at the end, blessed are the bank robbers.